Stenographic Transcript
Before the

COMMITTEE ON
ARMED SERVICES

UNITED STATES SENATE

HEARING TO RECEIVE TESTIMONY ON
UNITED STATES POLICY IN IRAQ AND SYRIA

Thursday, May 21, 2015

Washington, D.C.

Agenda

To receive testimony on United States policy in Iraq and Syria.

Table of Contents

Witnesses

1   HEARING TO RECEIVE TESTIMONY ON

2   UNITED STATES POLICY IN IRAQ AND SYRIA

3

4   Thursday, May 21, 2015

5

6   U.S. Senate

7   Committee on Armed Services

8   Washington, D.C.

9

10   The committee met, pursuant to notice, at 9:32 a.m. in

11   Room SD-G50, Dirksen Senate Office Building, Hon. John

12   McCain, chairman of the committee, presiding.

13   Committee Members Present: Senators McCain

14   [presiding], Inhofe, Ayotte, Cotton, Rounds, Ernst, Tillis,

15   Sullivan, Graham, Cruz, Reed, Nelson, Gillibrand,

16   Blumenthal, Donnelly, Kaine, and King.

17

18

19

20

21

22

23

24

25

1　　　　OPENING STATEMENT OF HON. JOHN McCAIN, U.S. SENATOR

2　FROM ARIZONA

3　　　　Chairman McCain: Now that Senator Ernst is here, we

4　can begin.

5　　　　[Laughter.]

6　　　　Chairman McCain: The committee meets today to receive

7　testimony on U.S. policy in Iraq and Syria.

8　　　　And I want to thank each of our expert witnesses for

9　appearing before us today on this critical and complex

10　topic.

11　　　　Before I go any further, the Secretary of Defense and

12　Chairman of the Joint Chiefs were invited to appear.

13　Admittedly, very short notice. And we will be asking them

14　to appear after the recess is over, depending on whether the

15　bill is on the floor, or not. But, we certainly would like

16　to hear from the Secretary of Defense and the Chairman of

17　the Joint Chiefs.

18　　　　Today, we have General Jack Keane, former Vice Chief of

19　Staff for the Army and chairman of the Institute for the

20　Study of War.

21　　　　And, General Keane, we're pleased you could take time

22　from your duties on FOX News to being with us today.

23　　　　Dr. Fred Kagan, who is -- that's a joke -- Dr. Fred

24　Kagan, director --

25　　　　[Laughter.]

1   Chairman McCain: Dr. Fred Kagan, the Director of the

2 Critical Threats Project at the American Enterprise

3 Institute; Colonel Derek Harvey, U.S. Army (Retired),

4 Director of the Global Initiative for Civil Society and

5 Conflict at the University of South Florida; and Brian

6 Katulis, who is a Senior Fellow at the Center for American

7 Progress.

8   Could I point out, for the benefit of my colleagues,

9 that General Keane and Dr. Kagan were key elements and

10 individuals who went over to the White House in 2006 to talk

11 to then-President George W. Bush concerning the need for a

12 surge, that -- the strategy in Iraq was failing at that

13 time, and they were two of the major architects -- and I

14 know they'll give credit to many others, but two of the

15 major architects of the surge, which turned out to be, at

16 great sacrifice of American blood and treasure, a success.

17   The black flags of ISIL are now flying over yet another

18 major Iraqi city, Ramadi, the capital of Iraq's Anbar

19 Province, and reports overnight suggest that ISIL now

20 controls the Syrian city of Palmyra, as well. This hearing

21 does not -- is not about the fall of any one city, as

22 important as those losses are, but, rather, what these

23 defeats have revealed about the limitations of an overly

24 constrained American air campaign, the weaknesses of Iraqi

25 forces, the growing malign role of Iran, and the

1   ineffectiveness and inadequacy of U.S. military support of

2   -- for our Iraqi and Syrian partners. But, most concerning,

3   it highlights the shortcomings of the administration's

4   indecisive policy, inadequate commitment, and incoherent

5   strategy. This misguided approach has failed to stop, if

6   not fostered, the expansion of ISIL to a dozen countries.

7   The loss of Ramadi, once the symbol of Iraqis working

8   together with brave young Americans in uniform to defeat al-

9   Qaeda, must be recognized as a significant defeat. ISIL's

10 victory gives it the appearance of strength and boosts its

11 ability to recruit more fighters while reinforcing Iran's

12 narrative that only it and its proxies can rescue Iraq.

13   The fall of Ramadi and capture by ISIL of American-

14 supplied military equipment is another setback for the

15 United States and further undermines our credibility as a

16 reliable strategic partner in the region.

17   And yet, the Obama administration seems unwilling or

18 unable to grasp the strategic significance. As ISIL

19 terrorists ransacked Ramadi -- by the way, the Pentagon's

20 news page ran a story with the headline, quote, "Strategy to

21 Defeat ISIL is Working." Secretary of State John Kerry said

22 Ramadi was a mere, quote, "target of opportunity." And 2

23 days ago, when a review should have been well underway to

24 correct an incoherent strategy that is woefully under-

25 resourced, the White House Press Secretary, Josh Ernst,

1   said, "Are we going to light our hair on fire every time

2   there's a setback?" I would point out for my colleagues

3   that maybe his hair isn't on fire, but there are bodies on

4   fire in the streets of Ramadi as we speak.

5   The disaster of Ramadi should lead to a complete

6   overhaul of U.S. Strategy. The President has stated, quote,

7   "Our goal is degrading and ultimately destroying ISIL," but

8   neither strategy nor resources support this goal. Our

9   efforts in Iraq may actually be aggravating the conditions

10 that gave rise to ISIL in the first place by relying on

11 brutal Iranian-backed Shi'a militias and insufficiently

12 empowering Sunni Iraqis. At best, this increases Iran's

13 malign influence. At worst, it reinforces ISIL's rhetoric

14 that it is the only force standing against violent sectarian

15 Iranian-backed militias.

16   President Obama has cleverly maneuvered us into the

17 position that Sunni Iraqis that we -- think we support Iran,

18 and Shi'a Iraqis think we support ISIL. But, the situation

19 is far worse in Syria. The Iran-backed Assad regime,

20 together with Iranian proxies like Hezbollah, continues the

21 slaughter that has killed more than 200,000 Syrians and

22 displaced 10 million more. Despite this tragedy, the

23 administration has defined its policy in Syria more by what

24 it will not do rather than the -- by the end state we aim to

25 achieve. Although the U.S. military's train-and-equip

1 program for moderate Syrian forces is now finally providing

2 assistance to vetted fighters, the administration still has

3 not decided whether it will defend Syrian opposition against

4 Assad's barrel bombs upon their return to Syria. Refusing

5 to support the forces we train is not only ineffective, it

6 is immoral.

7   While it is still unclear what President Obama is

8 willing to do in Syria, it is clear our partners do not draw

9 confidence from statements of what we will not do. Ramadi's

10 fall should lead our Nation's leaders to reconsider its

11 indecisive policy and incoherent strategy that has enabled

12 ISIL's expansion, undermined regional stability,

13 strengthened Iran, and harmed America's credibility. What

14 we desperately need is a comprehensive strategy, the

15 decisive application of an increased, but still limited,

16 amount of U.S. military power, and a concerted effort by the

17 Iraqi government to recruit, train, and equip Sunni forces.

18 This will require disciplined thinking, clear priorities, a

19 strategy supported by adequate resources, and, most of all,

20 the leadership and resolve of the President to succeed.

21   I look forward to hearing from our witnesses today on

22 these important questions.

23   Senator Reed.

24

25

         STATEMENT OF HON. JACK REED, U.S. SENATOR FROM RHODE
ISLAND

         Senator Reed: Well, first, let me thank the Chairman
for calling this timely and very, very important hearing,
and also thank Senator Nelson for acting as the Ranking
Member today. I have two Appropriations Committee -- one
Appropriations Committee and one Bank Committee markup, and
I apologize, I cannot be here.

         And, with that, with your permission, Mr. Chairman, I'd
like to yield to Senator Nelson.

         Chairman McCain: Senator Nelson.

1   STATEMENT OF HON. BILL NELSON, U.S. SENATOR FROM

2   FLORIDA

3   Senator Nelson: Thank you, Mr. Chairman.

4   And what I'm going to do is just put my statement in

5   the record so we can get on to it.

6   But, what you underscore is certainly accurate. The

7   fall of Ramadi -- what is the Abadi government going to do?

8   Do they have the capability of getting Sunnis to come in and

9   take up the fight against ISIS? And so, we need, as you all

10   testified to us -- How far are we along in implementing the

11   counter-ISIS campaign in Iraq? And what has the Abadi

12   government done to empower the Sunni tribes to resist ISIS?

13   And what does Ramadi mean about retaking Mosul? And will

14   these events force Iraq's political leadership to overcome

15   their differences in their attempts at government?

16   So, with those questions, thank you, Mr. Chairman.

17   [The prepared statement of Senator Nelson follows:]

18

19

20

21

22

23

24

25

1   Chairman McCain: Thank you, Senator Nelson.

2   And, you know, Palmyra is one of the historic places on

3   Earth, and, as it's being threatened now, we know what ISIS

4   does to these antiquities. We're about to perhaps,

5   unfortunately, see another destruction of an obviously

6   irreplaceable historic heritage sites that -- it would be

7   another great tragedy along the lines of the destruction of

8   the Buddhist statues at Bamiyan, years ago.

9   Welcome the witnesses.

10   And, General Keane, we'll begin with you. Thank you,

11 sir.

12

13

14

15

16

17

18

19

20

21

22

23

24

25

STATEMENT OF GENERAL JOHN M. KEANE, USA (RET.), FORMER
VICE CHIEF OF STAFF OF THE ARMY

General Keane: Thank you, Chairman McCain and Ranking
Member Reed and Senator Nelson, distinguished members of the
committee. Appreciate you inviting me back to testify.

I was here a few months ago dealing with global
security challenges facing the United States. And I must
say, I was pretty impressed with the bipartisan support for
the challenges our country is facing and the way you're
willing to work together to come to grips with it.

I'm honored to be here with my distinguished
colleagues. Obviously, I know Fred Kagan and Derek Harvey
very well. They're long and close associates. As much as
Fred and I may have had some impact on the previous
administration in changing their strategy -- and there were
others who were working towards that end, as well -- Derek
Harvey, sitting here, was the catalyst for understanding the
enemy. He was pushing against the intelligence group think
that existed at the time. And he defined that enemy better
than anybody did in this town. And that was the beginning
of understanding what was happening to us, why it was
happening, and what Fred and I thought we could
realistically do about it. So, I'm honored to be here with
all of them.

I've got some maps up there that you may want to use to

1　get a reference. It's always good to see where things are

2　happening, to understand the scale and magnitude.

3　　　　　You know, approximately 9 months ago, the President

4　announced the United States public policy --

5　　　　　Chairman McCain: General, could you give me a second?

6　I don't think we have --

7　　　　　General Keane: We've got to get the Chairman maps.

8　Okay.

9　　　　　Approximately 9 months ago, the President announced the

10　United States public policy that, along with our coalition

11　partners, the United States would degrade and ultimately

12　destroy ISIS. Weeks later, he changed "destroy ISIS" to

13　"defeat," a more appropriate term.

14　　　　　A strategy was crafted to accomplish this objective,

15　which consisted among some things as humanitarian

16　assistance, undermining the ISIS ideology, countering the

17　finances, providing military assistance to our Iraqi

18　partners, to include airstrikes into Syria, and assisting

19　the Iraqi government politically to move toward a more

20　representative government, which actually, obviously, led to

21　a change in governments. I cannot address undermining the

22　ideology and the finances in this testimony. It's beyond my

23　expertise.

24　　　　　While there has been some progress and some success,

25　looking at this strategy today, we know now that the

11

1   conceptual plan is fundamentally flawed. The resources

2   provided to support Iraq are far from adequate. The timing

3   and urgency to provide arms, equipment, and training is

4   insufficient. And, as such, we are not only failing, we

5   are, in fact, losing this war. Moreover, I can say with

6   certainty that this strategy will not defeat ISIS.

7   As to the concept, ISIS, who is headquartered in Syria,

8   recruits, trains, and resupplies in Syria, controls large

9   swaths of territory in Syria -- and you can look at your map

10   there to take a look at that -- to include the entire

11   Euphrates River Valley in Syria from Iraq to the Turkish

12   border. It connects now to the Euphrates River Valley in

13   Anbar Province, which leads to the suburbs of Baghdad. And

14   it's currently expanding to the west as far as Damascus.

15   And they just seized, as the Chairman mentioned, Palmyra

16   City and Palmyra Air Base in Central City -- in central

17   Syria, aligning the central east-west corridor from Iraq all

18   the way to homes in the west in Syria.

19   And yet -- and yet -- we have no strategy to defeat

20   ISIS in Syria. We have no ground force, which is the defeat

21   mechanism. Yes, we have airpower. And, despite the success

22   at Khobani -- and yes, we have degraded ISIS command and

23   control in Syria, their logistics, and we have killed many

24   ISIS fighters -- but, airpower would not defeat ISIS. It

25   has not been able to deny ISIS freedom of maneuver and the

1   ability to attack at will. Syria is ISIS's sanctuary. We

2   cannot succeed in Iraq if ISIS is allowed to maintain that

3   sanctuary in Syria. We need a strategy now to defeat ISIS

4   in Syria.

5   As you can see on the map that deals with the global

6   rings -- take a look at that -- many ISIS -- on that ISIS

7   map -- ISIS is expanding beyond Iraq and Syria into Sinai,

8   Yemen, Libya, and Afghanistan. This is where they actually

9   have people on the ground, and they have actually provided

10   resources, and they have -- actually have a contract written

11   and signed with the people on the ground who are affiliated

12   with them. And they're also inspiring and motivating

13   radical sympathizers throughout the world, which are

14   depicted in that map on yellow, as we are painfully aware of

15   in Europe and in the United States and Australia. Yet,

16   there is no strategy with our allies to counter that

17   expansion. I would go further to say there is no strategy

18   to counter the destabilization of the Middle East.

19   As to Iraq, it certainly makes sense to assist Iraq in

20   reclaiming lost territory and avoid deploying U.S. ground

21   combat units. However, ISIS, despite some setbacks, is on

22   the offense, with the ability to attack at will anyplace,

23   anytime. And, particularly, the fall of Ramadi has exposed

24   the weakness of the current Iraq strategy. It is more than

25   just a setback.

1   Politically, the administration deserves credit for

2   helping to usher out the Maliki government and bring the new

3   Abadi government in. However, Abadi is isolated, is

4   undermined by Maliki, who is still and remains a nefarious

5   character, and others within Abadi's own party. Abadi is

6   unduly influenced by Iran. And the United States is not

7   nearly as consequential as it should be. A U.S. objective

8   should be, politically, to reduce Iran's influence. We need

9   a focused diplomatic and political effort with the Abadi

10   government, with the best people we have available to do it.

11   Militarily, clearly the Iraqi army is a serious

12   problem. While some have fought heroically, many have not.

13   There are serious leadership, discipline, morale, and

14   competence issues. This will take time to fix. But, if we

15   believe that Iraq is important to U.S. security, then we

16   must help them fix it. And it will take many more trainers

17   and a much more concerted effort to put in the best leaders

18   available.

19   The Sunni tribal force is almost nonexistent, yet we

20   cannot reclaim the Sunni territory that has been lost,

21   particularly Anbar Province and Mosul, and we cannot hold

22   the territory after we have reclaimed it if we do not have a

23   Sunni tribal force. The Abadi government must authorize

24   this force, and the United States should arm, equip, and

25   train it. They must know that the Iraqi government and the

1   United States is behind them. Right now, they know the

2   Iraqi government is not. Their families are being killed by

3   the hundreds, eventually by the thousands. And they are

4   disillusioned by the United States, in terms of its lack of

5   support.

6   The Peshmerga. They're skilled, they're willed, they

7   will fight. They need arms, and they need advisors, down at

8   the fighting level, to assist them with planning, execution,

9   and to call in airstrikes.

10   The Shi'a militia are largely protecting Baghdad. Most

11 of what ISIS owns is Sunni territory. If we use the Shi'a

12 militia to reclaim that territory and hold it, Iran has

13 undue influence, politically, in Iraq as a result of it, and

14 the Sunni people will suffer under the hand and the gun of

15 the Shi'a militias. We must, in fact, reduce their

16 influence.

17   The role of advisors. Advisors are only at brigade

18 headquarters and above, currently. This is flawed. Advisor

19 teams must be with the units that are fighting, at least at

20 the battalion level, which is what we did in the past so

21 successfully. Advisors, as the name implies, helps units

22 plan and execute, and it also builds their confidence in

23 themselves. They are also forward air controllers and can

24 direct airpower as well as attack helicopters. The war in

25 Iraq is largely close-combat urban warfare, which demands

1   the bombs be guided from our airplanes to the ground by

2   people on the ground. Seventy-five percent of the sorties

3   that we're currently running with our attack aircraft come

4   back without dropping bombs, mostly because they cannot

5   acquire the target or properly identify the target. Forward

6   air controllers fix that problem.

7   Special Operation Forces direct-action teams should be

8   employed, not as an exception, which is what we successfully

9   saw this last weekend in Syria with the raid, but routinely

10 in Iraq and Syria against the ISIS leadership and critical

11 infrastructure. Similar to what we have done in Iraq and

12 Afghanistan in the past during the surges, when Fred and I

13 were there, as well as Colonel Harvey, we averaged -- the

14 surges in Iraq and Afghanistan, we averaged somewhere

15 between eight to ten of these operations a night. In fact,

16 when the UBL raid was taking place in Pakistan, there were

17 nine of these going on in Afghanistan that very night.

18   We should also do large-scale raids. What does that

19 mean? We should use elements like Rangers to conduct

20 attacks at night over critical infrastructure to kill ISIS

21 fighters who are difficult to dig out with airpower at

22 altitude. These are surprise attacks. They're not intended

23 to stay. They're in and out maybe one night. We stay, at

24 the most, a couple of days, depending on how much of a fight

25 we're getting into.

1   We desperately need enablers to assist the Iraqi

2 Security Forces. This is crucial support that helps them

3 succeed on the battlefield. What is it? Robust

4 intelligence capability. We have some, but we've got to

5 ramp it up more than what we have. Increased UAVs, not to

6 assist airpower, which we're currently doing in terms of

7 surveillance, but to assist ground forces. That's a

8 different application, and it's a different type of UAV. We

9 need attack aviation. That's Apache helicopters. And we

10 need other helicopters to assist the ground forces. C-130

11 transports to move troops and supplies and other logistics

12 support. And we need increased U.S. command-and-control

13 headquarters to help control the increase of trainers,

14 advisors, and others that I'm suggesting here.

15   Obviously, what I am suggesting is increased U.S.

16 political and military involvement in Iraq, which begins to

17 shore up many of the weaknesses of the current strategy.

18 While I believe we can still do this without U.S. and allied

19 combat brigades, it is much more difficult now than what it

20 was 9 months ago. I believe we have to do some serious

21 contingency planning for the introduction of ground combat

22 brigades, both U.S. and allied.

23   Finally, we need to get past our political psychosis on

24 Iraq which is defined by the questions: Should the United

25 States have gone into Iraq in 2003? Should the United

1   States left Iraq in 2011? While they were crucial U.S.

2   policy decisions, there is -- and there is much to learn

3   from them, and we have -- we've got to get past it. ISIS is

4   much more than Iraq. Our forces should be what the -- our

5   focus should be what the President started out with:

6   defeating ISIS. That will take political will. And war is

7   a test of wills. It will take accepting risk. It will take

8   accepting casualties. It will take focus. And it will take

9   increased U.S. resources. And it will take honest

10 evaluations as -- and assessments.

11   What I fear is this. I hear a disturbing and

12 frightening echo of the summer of 2006, when administration,

13 senior government -- when a different administration, senior

14 government officials, and military senior generals came

15 before this committee and, in the face of compelling

16 evidence that our strategy in Iraq was failing, these

17 officials looked at you and defended that strategy and told

18 you that, overall, the strategy was succeeding. You and

19 your predecessors took a strong bipartisan exception to

20 those opinions. Many, as a result of it, wanted to give up

21 on Iraq. Others wanted to do something about fixing the

22 problem.

23   I hope you choose the latter and get on with helping to

24 fix the problem. And I look forward to your questions.

25   Thank you.

1   [The prepared statement of General Keane follows:]
2
3
4
5
6
7
8
9
10
11
12
13
14
15
16
17
18
19
20
21
22
23
24
25

```
 1       Chairman McCain:   Dr. Kagan.

 2

 3

 4

 5

 6

 7

 8

 9

10

11

12

13

14

15

16

17

18

19

20

21

22

23

24

25
```

1 STATEMENT OF DR. FREDERICK W. KAGAN, CHRISTOPHER

2 DELMUTH CHAIR AND DIRECTOR, CRITICAL THREATS PROJECT,

3 AMERICAN ENTERPRISE INSTITUTE

4   Dr. Kagan: Mr. Chairman, Senator Nelson, thank you

5 very much for calling this hearing. And thank so many of

6 you for attending. It shows a sense of urgency about the

7 problem on the part of this committee that it's hard to

8 detect in the rest of the administration. So, I'm very

9 grateful to the committee, as always, for the opportunity to

10 speak, but for the attention that it's trying to focus on

11 this problem.

12   I receive, every day, a superb daily rollup of

13 activities in the region produced by my team in the Critical

14 Threats Project and the team at the Institute for the Study

15 of War. I can't read it all anymore. It's too long. It's

16 too long because the region is engulfed in war. It's sort

17 of hard to tell that from the isolated headlines that pop up

18 and fade away. But, we -- this is the regional war. This

19 is the beginning of the regional war. It could get a lot

20 worse, but this is a war that is becoming a sectarian war

21 across the region. It is a war between Saudi Arabia and

22 Iran, fought largely by proxies, but now, dismayingly, also

23 directly. There are some people who think that it's a good

24 thing that the Saudis and others are acting independently.

25 I would suggest that they take a look at the historical

1   efficacy of Saudi military forces and ask themselves if they

2   think that that's really a reed we want to rest our weight

3   on.

4   And I think we can focus too heavily on what the Iraqi

5   Security Forces are doing, or not doing, as we have in the

6   past. They're not doing enough. Prime Minister Abadi is in

7   a box. We have helped put him there with our policies. So,

8   it's not sufficient just to look at and criticize what the

9   Iraqis are doing. We really do need to look in a mirror and

10   look at what we are doing or not doing.

11   As I follow the daily reports, I see a coherent enemy

12   strategy across the region. I see deliberate enemy

13   operations, which you can actually depict on a map. And I

14   commend to you a terrific report by the Institute for the

15   Study of War called "ISIS Captures Ramadi," which actually

16   has a military -- old-fashioned military-style map showing

17   the ISIS maneuvers, because they are maneuvering. This is

18   not a terrorist organization. This is an army that is

19   conducting military maneuvers on an operational level with a

20   great deal of skill. It is not an accident that Ramadi fell

21   over the weekend and Palmyra fell yesterday. It is not an

22   accident that there were ISIS attacks in Beiji and at the

23   refinery, that there was a prison break in Diyala, that

24   there were threats against the -- not the Hajj -- a

25   pilgrimage in Baghdad, and then Ramadi was decisively

1   attacked and taken. This was a coherent campaign plan, and

2   a very intelligent one, very well executed. This is a

3   serious threat. What I can't discern from the daily

4   operations, let alone from the statements of the

5   administration, is any coherent American strategy to respond

6   to this threat.

7   And I want to talk about the threat for a minute. ISIS

8   is one of the most evil organizations that has ever existed

9   in the world. We really have to reckon with that. This is

10   not a minor annoyance. This is not a group that maybe we

11   can negotiate with down the road someday. This is a group

12   that is committed to the destruction of everything decent in

13   the world. And the evidence of that is the wanton

14   destruction, uncalled for even by their own ideology,

15   frankly, of antiquities thousands of years old that

16   represent the heart of the emergence of human civilization

17   in the West. This is a group that sells captives into

18   slavery. It's a major source of financing for them,

19   actually. This is a room -- a group that engages

20   deliberately in mass rape. This is a group that conducts

21   mass murder. And this is a group that is calling for and

22   condoning and supporting and encouraging lone-wolf attacks,

23   and it will soon, I think, not be just lone-wolf attacks, in

24   the United States and the West. This is a group of

25   unfathomable evil. And, unfortunately, they are extremely

1   effective. And they have a degree of military capability --

2   not terrorist capability -- that we have not seen before in

3   an al-Qaeda organization. This is not something where we

4   should be spectators. This is not something where we should

5   just say, as some people do, "Well, just let them kill each

6   other." This is unacceptable, from a moral perspective and

7   from a U.S. national security perspective, to just watch a

8   group like this succeed in this way.

9   I want to make the point that, of course, any criticism

10   of the White House today is received -- at least from our

11   side -- is received as a partisan attack. And I want to

12   make the point that if that was the case, then I must have

13   been a Democrat in 2006, because we were attacking the Bush

14   administration with the Senator -- with the Chairman and a

15   number of other members of the committee, as aggressively,

16   or, in fact, more aggressively, than we've ever critiqued

17   this White House. The fact is that what matters is that the

18   strategy is failing, as it was failing in 2006, only we are

19   in a much worse strategic position today than we ever were

20   in 2006, because it's not just Iraq.

21   I note that, to speak of the issue of urgency, the

22   Iranians seem to feel a certain sense of urgency about this,

23   as well. And their Minister of Defense, General Dehghan,

24   was in Baghdad over the last few days, signing defense

25   cooperation agreements, ostensibly, but surely working to

1 coordinate Iranian support on the ground. The Foreign

2 Policy Advisor to the Supreme Leader, Velayati, was in

3 Damascus and Beirut, talking with Bashar al-Assad and Hassan

4 Nasrallah, no doubt coordinating plans to, I assume,

5 maintain and increase the military deployment of Hezbollah

6 forces in Syria and possibly ask Assad what his plan is,

7 given the circumstances. Those are very senior leaders. I

8 don't notice that we have sent senior leaders of that rank,

9 or anything close to it, to speak with Prime Minister Abadi.

10 And, of course, we have no one to speak with, effectively,

11 in Syria.

12 Senator Nelson asked about what this means for the

13 counter-ISIS campaign. It means that the campaign that has

14 been described by the administration and our general

15 officers is completely derailed. I do not believe that

16 there is any reasonable prospect that it will be possible to

17 retake Mosul this year. I think the fight for Ramadi will

18 be hard enough. I think that these operations in and around

19 Ramadi demonstrate that the Iraqi Security Forces, at

20 current levels of U.S. support, are not capable even of

21 defending their territory against determined ISIS attack,

22 let alone clearing a major ISIS safe haven.

23 So, we are -- our campaign strategy is completely

24 derailed, in my view. I think it was a campaign strategy,

25 as the Chairman pointed out, that was of limited likelihood

1   to be successful, in any event, because it addressed only

2   part of the problem and left a major safe haven effectively

3   untouched. But, such as it was, it's over.

4   My colleague, Derek Harvey, will speak in some more

5   detail about what kinds of troops and enablers are required.

6   I agree with General Keane -- I'm even willing to put a

7   number on the table -- I think that we need to have a total

8   of 15- to 20,000 U.S. troops in Iraq in order to provide the

9   necessary enablers, advisors, and so forth. I think

10   anything less than that is simply unserious.

11   And I think we really need to do that, because, I

12   think, otherwise, we're looking at an ISIS state that is

13   going to persist. We're looking at an ISIS state that is

14   going to continue to govern territory, that is going to

15   continue to have resources that we simply cannot afford to

16   let an evil enemy of this variety have. And I think it is a

17   major U.S. national security priority to respond to this,

18   especially as it's become clear that it's beyond the

19   capabilities of the Iraqis.

20   And lastly, I want to make two larger points that are

21   directly relevant to this committee. One is, you cannot

22   argue for a forceful strategy in Iraq and defend the

23   sequester. Our Armed Forces have been seriously damaged by

24   the sequester. It needs to be removed immediately. In

25   fact, the Armed Forces budget needs to be increased

1 significantly. We are at war, whether we like it or not,

2 and the longer this President refuses to address it, the

3 worse it's going to be when we become engaged. We need to

4 be preparing for that now.

5   And lastly, we need to be strengthening our abilities

6 to collect intelligence, and not weakening them. This is

7 not the moment to dismantle our capabilities to see what the

8 enemy is doing. This is the moment to be engaged in wise

9 reform of oversight of the intelligence community. And so,

10 It is ironic that one of your colleagues spent yesterday

11 arguing for the elimination of a program important to our

12 national security.

13   So, I think there are things that the administration

14 can do and things that Congress can do, but it's going to be

15 a tough fight.

16   I thank the committee for listening to me this morning.

17   [The prepared statement of Dr. Kagan follows:]

18   [COMMITTEE INSERT]

19

20

21

22

23

24

25

1   Chairman McCain: Colonel Harvey.

2

3

4

5

6

7

8

9

10

11

12

13

14

15

16

17

18

19

20

21

22

23

24

25

1   STATEMENT OF COLONEL DEREK J. HARVEY, USA (RET.),

2   DIRECTOR, GLOBAL INITIATIVE FOR CIVIL SOCIETY AND CONFLICT,

3   UNIVERSITY OF SOUTH FLORIDA

4   Colonel Harvey: Mr. Chairman, Senator Nelson, and

5   members of the committee, thank you for having me here. I

6   appreciate the opportunity.

7   I want to begin with focusing on the Islamic State and

8   the trends in Iraq. I believe that, even before the fall of

9   Ramadi, the best that could be said is that Baghdad was

10   holding the line. Even with the success in Tikrit, there's

11   great difficulty in holding that terrain. And even in areas

12   that have been cleared earlier in northern Diyala Province

13   in eastern Saladin, ISIS has worked their way back in. They

14   just changed their profile, went to ground, and now they're

15   infiltrating back in and conducting attacks and rebuilding

16   their capabilities.

17   Over the past month, they've continued to do shaping

18   operations in the Baghdad area, western Baghdad. In one

19   day, just a couple of days ago, there were eight IEDs, two

20   VBIEDs, and several small-arms skirmishes in Baghdad itself.

21   That's to say nothing about what's going on in Abu Ghraib

22   and other areas around the belts of Baghdad.

23   They continue to hold the line along the Kurdish front,

24   north in the Nineveh area around Mosul, and they've expanded

25   successfully in other areas, particularly in Syria. They

1   are very good at doing shaping operations. They are taking

2   advantage of their interior lines of communication. They

3   are well armed, well resourced, and well led.

4   I think the fall of Ramadi should lead to questions

5   about the progress asserted by the Pentagon and the

6   administration. There are two strategically important Sunni

7   Arab cities in Iraq: Mosul, the second largest city, which

8   was a former Ottoman capital, and, of course, Ramadi, which

9   is the capital of the largest geographic province. And ISIS

10   controls Raqqa, which is another provincial capital, but

11   it's in Syria. The fall of Ramadi renews the sense that

12   ISIS has momentum, which is important for rallying Sunni

13   Arabs who may be on the fence in this fight, and also could

14   aid with foreign fighter recruitment and some funding.

15   without an alternative, Sunni Arabs, tribes, and the

16   peoples in the region, without someone to protect them and

17   lead them, are going to fall into the camp of the Islamic

18   State, particularly as this campaign becomes increasingly

19   polarized. And the movement of Shi'a militias, Popular

20   Mobilization units, into Anbar Province is going to

21   contribute to this polarization. And I fully expect that

22   the Islamic State, in the near future, will try to conduct

23   operations in Karbala and Najaf to further inflame this

24   fight. That is part of their major strategy, to polarize

25   this fight between the different communities.

1   Now, I would note that ISIS has many challenges and

2 weaknesses, but the problem is that ISIS is not losing. I

3 believe that the U.S. has continued to underestimate the

4 Islamic State, which I suspect shows a lack of understanding

5 about the Islamic State, its capabilities, strengths, and

6 weaknesses and how it sees the fight and a path to victory.

7   We've seen this story before. It's like deja vu, for

8 me. We focus too much on our own activity, our own

9 programs, our own budgets, but we're not focusing on the

10 impact on the enemy. And the enemy has a vote.

11   From public statements, we're not looking at the right

12 things, and the metrics and measures that are asserted by

13 the military, the Pentagon, are not really appropriate. The

14 number of airstrikes is interesting, but irrelevant. What

15 is the effect on the enemy and its capacity to fight?

16 Stating that ISIS has lost 25 percent of the territory it

17 conquered is interesting, but it's really not relevant,

18 because ISIS did not control eastern Saladin or northern

19 Diyala or some of the other areas, but they're still there.

20 They're contesting, and they're rebuilding, and they're

21 shaping. So, that is a false metric that's been put out.

22   Striking oil infrastructure in Syria is a good thing,

23 and it's been degraded. But, the enemy has a vote. It's --

24 their efforts there have been complicated. They've reduced

25 their production. But, they've adapted, and, creatively,

1   they have developed miniature mobile refinement

2   capabilities, even using blow-dryer air heaters to make

3   refined product. It is crude, yet it is a sophisticated

4   adaptation. And crude is still going to Turkey. And they

5   are producing enough fuel for their own requirements.

6   They're still earning millions of dollars every month from

7   oil in Syria. It's been degraded, but I think the lower

8   cost of oil on the markets has had just as much of an impact

9   as any operations we've conducted. And again, they have

10   adapted.

11   The same for funding and foreign fighter flow. They

12   are still very resilient and adaptive in working around the

13   actions that have been taken. And the actions that have

14   been taken on foreign fighter flow and going after finances

15   have been weak and not very assertive, not well resourced.

16   And I'll talk more about that.

17   ISIS is excelling at a hybrid war. They're fighting

18   conventionally, as needed, they're adapting, and they're

19   employing terrorist techniques -- coercion, assassination,

20   subversion -- as necessary, depending upon the terrain. It

21   is showing that it can hold key terrain, fight hard, and

22   synchronize operations across space and time. And they

23   respond with agility to secure tactical and operational

24   advantages and overmatch, as we saw in Ramadi. They are

25   very effective, they are well led. They are skilled, and

1   they have professional-quality leadership and command-and-

2   control. And they know the geography, they know the

3   terrain, and they know the human terrain in these areas

4   very, very, very well. They are ruthless, and they are

5   committed and determined. And they're exhibiting the will

6   to fight. And they're fighting for power, they're fighting

7   for ideological reasons, but, for many Sunni Arabs who are

8   frustrated and angered about their condition in life and how

9   they have been treated by Baghdad, they're fighting for

10 their land, their families, and their future. And they are

11 not motivated by a hardline Salafist Takfiri annihilationist

12 agenda, but they're fighting anyway, because they're

13 fighting for their own lives and their own future, and

14 they're fearful.

15   There are many Sunni military-aged males, to date, that

16 have not taken sides in this fight. It's just a matter of

17 time, if this polarization continues and we let this drag

18 on, that ISIS will gain more and more recruits from the

19 Iraqi population base. The Iraqi fight with ISIS is not

20 dominated by foreign fighters. This is a homegrown fight,

21 and we have to keep that in mind. ISIS, as Fred mentioned,

22 maintains operational freedom in most of the Sunni Arab

23 provinces, and they appear stronger because, importantly,

24 relatively, their opposition is very weak.

25   Now, the Sunni Arab political and tribal leaders are

1   weak and divided, and seen as illegitimate by many within

2   these Sunni Arab provinces. And too many Sunni Arabs are on

3   the fence. They've been given no reason to come onto the

4   side of the Baghdad government or to come to us. Prime

5   Minister Abadi's government is weak and divided, and is

6   increasingly undermined by Shi'a opposition. Same with the

7   Iraqi Security Forces that are small, weak, poorly

8   resourced, and not well led. And it will take far too long

9   to train and rebuild them to make a difference this year.

10   Moreover, I assess that there is a concerted effort to

11   undermine the efficacy of the Iraqi Security Forces by Shi'a

12   militias, Iranian proxies, and some members within the

13   government, including the Dawa Party, particularly some

14   members in the Ministry of Interior. They seek to weaken

15   the Iraqi Security Forces and provide alternative

16   institutions of power that they control.

17   And again, the coalition is weak. And we could talk

18   about that. But, there's not a lot of allied cooperation

19   and resources put into this fight.

20   And lastly, the U.S. lines of operation, for the most

21   part, have been poorly resourced, both in theater and at the

22   interagency level right here in Washington, D.C. I do not

23   see the urgency or the resourcing within Treasury or the

24   intelligence community or others to really energy and

25   aggressively go after this fight in this region.

1   So, although U.S. airstrikes, I believe, have

2   complicated the ISIS operations, the air campaign has not

3   been decisive. It's been relatively small and limited. And

4   the Islamic State, as I mentioned, has been adaptive and

5   creative. Importantly, they remain well armed and well

6   resourced. And our lines of operation, be it counter-

7   finance, counter-foreign-fighter flow, delegitimizing the

8   brand, the training, building of the ISF, and the military

9   campaign, at best, appear disjointed, poorly resourced, and

10   lack an effective framework to bring it all together. I

11   think we need to relook this.

12   And, with that, I'll look forward to your questions.

13   [The prepared statement of Colonel Harvey follows:]

14   [COMMITTEE INSERT]

15

16

17

18

19

20

21

22

23

24

25

```
 1      Chairman McCain:   Thank you.

 2      Mr. Katulis, thank you for being here.

 3

 4

 5

 6

 7

 8

 9

10

11

12

13

14

15

16

17

18

19

20

21

22

23

24

25
```

1   STATEMENT OF BRIAN KATULIS, SENIOR FELLOW, CENTER FOR

2   AMERICAN PROGRESS

3   Mr. Katulis: Great. Thank you, Mr. Chairman and

4   Senator Nelson and all of your distinguished colleagues.

5   It's a real honor to be here today.

6   Mr. Chairman, your efforts, over the last few months,

7   to elevate our national security debate have been incredible

8   and very important, the hearings that you held earlier this

9   year and everything that the members of the committee have

10 been doing have been very important for our country as we

11 look at the world and not just the Middle East.

12   Mr. Chairman, I prepared written testimony. With your

13 permission, I'd like to submit that for the record --

14   Chairman McCain: Without objection.

15   Mr. Katulis: -- this afternoon.

16   And it's really an honor, here, to be with the

17 copanelists, who I have great respect for, not only their

18 expertise, but their service to country. And what I wanted

19 to do this morning with my remarks is to try to complement

20 their insights with what I focus on in my own work, which is

21 looking at dynamics within the region and the strategic

22 dynamics, and nesting the problem of Iraq, Syria, and ISIS

23 within that. And, Mr. Chairman, you said, at the outset,

24 beforehand, that you'd like to discuss concrete steps. So,

25 while I give my analysis of what I think is happening in

1   Iraq, Syria, the region, and more broadly, I will offer some

2   ideas that I hope we can discuss, some of which I think

3   members of the panel have proposed in legislation.

4   The way I see the challenge -- and I don't disagree

5   with much of what was said here earlier -- the challenge of

6   ISIS, I think, operates on three different levels, or three

7   concentric circles:

8   The first is Iraq and Syria, quite obviously. That's

9   where the devastation has been astounding over the last few

10   years. And many of the steps, I think, that have been

11   proposed here, in terms of security measures and security

12   cooperation measures, is something that I, frankly -- it's a

13   little outside of my expertise to evaluate. I look at the

14   political and strategic dynamics. But, I do think, inside

15   of Iraq, no matter what we've done or what we do in the

16   coming years, every type of security assistance should be

17   implemented with a close eye to internal political and power

18   dynamics. And, at this stunning moment -- and what happened

19   in Ramadi, I think, should shock everybody -- we should keep

20   an eye on these measures of what we need to do to help our

21   Iraqi partners on the security front, but understand what we

22   have learned over the last 10 years plus, is that the

23   political dynamics are terribly important.

24   In those regards, what I think we need to do and the

25   Obama administration needs to do is to hold the Iraqi

1 government accountable for a lot of the ideas that have been

2 discussed, in terms of arming Sunni tribes, building a

3 national guard. If you look at what the Obama

4 administration did last summer -- and I was a supporter of

5 this measure of using security assistance as leverage to

6 help the Iraqis create a different type of Iraqi government

7 -- we need to continue that process. When the police in

8 Ramadi were not being funded, when concepts like the

9 national guard still remain stuck in parliament, it makes it

10 hard for any number of U.S. trainers to actually do their

11 job if those mechanisms are in place.

12   A second thing I think we need to start to entertain --

13 and I know people are discussing this -- is the notion of

14 greater decentralization inside of Iraq, decentralization of

15 authority, in some of the proposals that people have

16 discussed about mechanisms for giving arms directly to Sunni

17 tribes or to Kurdish forces. Again, I think we should

18 consider that and balance it against the overall objective

19 of trying to keep Iraq together.

20   The second component, obviously, is Syria. And this,

21 in my view, is the weakest link in the overall approach in

22 this first circle. And Mr. Chairman, Senator Kaine, many

23 others, have highlighted this, but we need to do something

24 about this. The gap between the Obama administration's

25 stated goals and what we're actually doing to shape the

1   environment on the ground is alarming. In my view, we need

2   to accelerate that which the administration proposed and you

3   funded, the training and equipping of third-way forces. We

4   need to link these efforts to the broader regional dynamics.

5   What's happening in Syria right now is a very complicated

6   engagement by actors in the region. If you see not only

7   ISIS's gains, but the gains of Jabhat al-Nusra, al-Qaeda's

8   front, this -- these gains don't come from nowhere. They're

9   being offered support from various actors in the region.

10 And the main point is that the end state in Syria, which is

11 often described by the administration in ways that our

12 tactics don't link up with what we want to achieve.

13   But, the overall point in this first circle -- Iraq and

14 Syria -- which I hope you take away and I think we need to

15 discuss some more, is, How do you link these problems and

16 how we address them? What worries me is that, quite often,

17 we look at a challenge in Iraq, or a corner of Iraq, but we

18 don't link it to the broader problem of Iraq and Syria.

19 Last summer, ISIS effectively eroded the borders between

20 these two countries. And what we've had over the last year

21 or so is a debate about a series of different tactics, some

22 of which have been implemented, and some have not. And I

23 think if we can all bring our thinking together to talk

24 about, How do we actually have an integrated strategy that

25 focuses on ISIS, both in Iraq and Syria?

1   On the second level, the regional level -- and here I

2   hope we can think a little bit more about this -- but, for

3   essentially the last 4 or 5 years, the Middle East has

4   slipped into this period of fragmentation. Not only has

5   Iraq and Syrian state structures collapsed, we've seen Libya

6   and Yemen feel these strains. And a big part of what is

7   going on -- and this challenge of ISIS and where it comes

8   from -- is the struggle between the regional powers: Iran

9   and Saudi Arabia, but there are other actors, too. Much of

10   it is sectarian, but the conflict is multidimensional. It

11   is multifaceted. Our resources matter, but Iran, Saudi

12   Arabia, others, have been funding their own proxies. And

13   what I think is missing, in terms of the U.S. leadership on

14   all of this, is accounting for all of these efforts. How do

15   we actually better organize and come up with a better

16   strategic conception?

17   Essentially, since 2003 and the Iraq War, when we made

18   the decision to move from a strategic posture of dual

19   containment of Iran and Iraq, I think we've been struggling

20   for: What is our overarching strategy in the Middle East?

21   We made some gains at certain periods, as was noted, in the

22   surge in Iraq in 2007-2008, but the broader picture of "What

23   is the United States trying to do in the region?" -- I

24   think, still that question has not been answered.

25   I think the Obama administration, rightfully, has taken

1   some positive steps in the right direction. The building of

2   an anti-ISIL coalition that has 62 countries in it,

3   including key stakeholders in the region, is an important

4   opportunity, one that I don't think has been fully seized

5   yet by the administration. Its engagements in that

6   coalition effort has been episodic. In February, for

7   instance, we had a Countering Violent Extremism Summit. And

8   the questions of "What then, after the summit?" I think

9   remain unanswered, to a large extent.

10   Just last week was a very important summit with the GCC

11   nations and, I think, an important communique. As with

12   everything in life, and with this administration, the

13   followup is going to be very important. Those commitments,

14   not only to Iraq and the fight in Syria, but the broader

15   fight against ISIS, there needs to be implementation.

16   And finally, one last point on the equilibrium point,

17   because I know it's a big debate up here, is the question of

18   equilibrium in the broader region. The Obama administration

19   often speaks of its engagement with Iran and the diplomatic

20   engagement on the nuclear front as an opportunity to achieve

21   some new type of equilibrium in the region. And I share

22   that aspiration. But, we need to be clear-eyed about how

23   hard that will be at a time when Iran, when other actors in

24   the region, are actually investing in a number of different

25   proxy wars. We need to be clear about how realistic that is

1   and what we're trying to do.

2   And on the final point, on the international level --

3   and I'll close here -- quite clearly, this problem of ISIS

4   is connected in ways that the problems that Derek and

5   General Keane and Dr. Kagan dealt with in the previous

6   decade -- it's much more complicated by the fact that you

7   have more than 15,000 foreign fighters flooding into -- and

8   perhaps the number is higher. And what I would suggest, at

9   the international level and our analysis, is that the debate

10   about ISIS is terribly important, but it's moving very

11   quickly. The debate that many people are having on Syria

12   right now is the fight between Jabhat al-Nusra, ISIL, and a

13   number of different actors. And I would say that 14 years

14   after 9/11, nearly 14 years, if you look at this broader

15   landscape, beyond Iraq and Syria, and Iraq and Syria as the

16   epicenter, this new trend toward Salafist jihadism, and the

17   growth of it, is something that we actually haven't wrestled

18   with, that we need to widen the landscape and keep focused

19   on it to assess what we're doing and whether we're applying

20   resources to meet those threats.

21   So, in conclusion, I hope the events of the last week

22   or so and, I hope our discussion today, is a constructive

23   wake-up call about what we can do to move from what I think

24   has been a largely reactive crisis management and somewhat

25   tactical approach to the problem set, not only over the last

1   year or two, but over the last decade. And I hope that the

2   events can motivate all of us, including you, with your

3   leadership, to drive towards the sorts of unity that we need

4   in things like an Authorization for the Use of Military

5   Force, a national conversation that reinvigorates our sense

6   of purpose. Because, as Derek and others have described,

7   this is a very dangerous adversary. We've not yet created

8   that strategy, the holistic strategy to actually defeat

9   them. And we can.

10   Thank you.

11   [The prepared statement of Mr. Katulis follows:]

12   [COMMITTEE INSERT]

13

14

15

16

17

18

19

20

21

22

23

24

25

1   Chairman McCain: Well, I thank you.

2   Could I mention to my colleagues that a vote is on,

3   and, if you'd like to go and come back, please do so. I'll

4   try to continue the hearing. I may have to pause. But, I

5   know that you have questions for the panel, so maybe we

6   could work it that way, however you'd like.

7   And I'd like to begin by picking up a little bit on

8   what Mr. Katulis just said. And this is this whole idea of

9   the perception of Iran and what the prospects are. Because

10   it seems to me that -- and the necessity to be clear-eyed

11   about it -- because it seems to me that one of the reasons

12   why we were not acting more aggressively against Bashar

13   Assad has got to do with this idea -- or, in my view,

14   illusion -- that once we conclude the nuclear agreement,

15   there will be a whole new relationship with Iran in the

16   Middle East, which, in my conversations with our friends in

17   the Sunni Arab states, scares the heck out of them.

18   And so, I -- maybe I could ask the panel about -- it

19   seems to me, in my view, that it is a real impediment to any

20   real significant action in Syria. For example, the Free

21   Syrian Army, what little there is that we are training, we

22   have not told -- or, the administration has said there is no

23   policy yet about, when we send these young men that we are

24   training back into Syria, that -- whether we would protect

25   them from Bashar Assad's barrel bombing. It seems to me

1   that that -- that there's a degree of immorality associated

2   with telling people you're going to train and equip them,

3   and then not protect them from being killed when they go

4   back in, and that they are only to fight ISIS and not Bashar

5   Assad, the father of ISIS.

6   So, I'd maybe begin with you, General Keane, and --

7   because it -- I don't think that Americans are fully aware

8   of this contradiction, here.

9   General Keane: Yeah. Well, Senator, I agree, in

10 principle, here, with what you're saying.

11   Just a -- so, our audience and the committee can

12 understand, we may forget that, early on in the rebellion

13 against Assad, the momentum was actually on the opposition-

14 forces side. Many people in this town were predicting that

15 the regime was going to fall. I think we can all recall

16 that.

17   Chairman McCain: That was testimony before this

18 committee by the Secretary of Defense and the Chairman of

19 the Joint Chiefs of Staff, yes.

20   General Keane: And that opposition force came to town

21 here and got many on their dance card to -- they needed

22 additional arms and ammunition -- specifically, antitank

23 weapons and antiaircraft weapons -- to deal with a

24 conventional military. They were stuck with rifles, machine

25 guns, RPGs, and the like. That early encounter in 2012 was

1   denied -- late 2011, early 2012. And then the CIA became

2   convinced that we could actually vet the Free Syrian Army --

3   and I will say that the Institute for the Study of War had

4   some impact on providing them information that assisted them

5   with that conclusion. And General Petraeus would have met

6   that, when he -- as the Director at the time. And he

7   presented a briefing to Secretaries Clinton and Panetta and

8   Dempsey -- General Dempsey -- and they agreed with him that

9   it was -- this force could, in fact, be armed, equipped, and

10   trained robustly. But, the administration did not do that.

11   And, tragically, as a result of that, the Free Syrian Army

12   now is a mere shadow of its former self. There's, frankly,

13   not much of it left.

14   Chairman McCain: And could I add --

15   General Keane: Go ahead.

16   Chairman McCain: -- in desperation, isn't it true that

17   they have now joined forces with al-Nusra, an al-Qaeda-

18   affiliated organization. Is that true?

19   General Keane: Well, organizations that were a part of

20   their organization, you know, have broken from them. They

21   were Islamic organizations, not radicalized, and they have

22   joined with Jabhat al-Nusra, who is -- who has gained more

23   territories, more aggressive, and has had more success

24   against the regime than any force out there. So, that is

25   true.

1   And what we're doing is -- and I know the committee's

2 been briefed on this -- we're attempting to train 5,000

3 people that would become part of the Free Syrian Army. But,

4 what organization are they going to plug into? And it's

5 totally disconnected, because the Free Syrian Army is not

6 fighting ISIS. They don't have the wherewithal to fight

7 ISIS and the regime. They're fighting the regime. So,

8 we're training forces that will join Free Syrian Army, in

9 theory. And, indeed, they will fight the regime forces,

10 which has nothing to do with ISIS, at the moment. So,

11 that's how flawed the strategy is in Syria. It makes no

12 sense. We don't have ground forces.

13   And, as the Chairman suggests, Does it make any sense

14 to train these forces, arm them and equip them and provide

15 them some leadership, and then put them back into the fight

16 against Assad's conventional military, which will bomb them

17 and attack them with conventional artillery, mortars, and,

18 obviously, barrel bombs and the like?

19   So, that strategy in Syria is flawed. And obviously,

20 the only way that ISIS will eventually be defeated in Syria

21 is with some kind of a ground force. Our allies in the

22 region are suggesting to us -- and we having -- we're not

23 agreeing with them -- is that what we should do is deal with

24 Assad, change the momentum against Assad by shutting down

25 his airpower, using no-fly zones and buffer zones to achieve

1   that end, and that change in military -- in momentum,

2   militarily on the battlefield can shift the political

3   equation to get some kind of a settlement.

4   Now, listen, that's arguable whether that's achievable,

5   or not. But, sitting here and doing nothing, and permitting

6   this to go on, I think that's quite irresponsible, in terms

7   of the humanitarian catastrophe that's taking place there,

8   and also that ISIS is expanding and gaining in strength in

9   Syria every single week and month.

10   So, the Syrian strategy needs to be thought out. It

11   needs to lead to a situation where we have our Arab -- where

12   we have a coalition of Arabs in the region, and possibly the

13   Turks participating also. And they would likely ask us to

14   participate in a coalition to deal with ISIS in Syria. And

15   I do think we should listen to them about dealing with Assad

16   and that regime first, in some limited capacity, to change

17   the political equation.

18   Chairman McCain: I'm going to have to go vote. I'd

19   like to hear the -- from the other witnesses. I'm going to

20   have to go vote.

21   Senator Ernst.

22   And if someone isn't back yet after you, we will take a

23   brief pause until my return.

24   Senator Ernst: Thank you, Mr. Chair.

25   Thank you, gentlemen, for being here today. I really

1   do appreciate it very much. And I apologize that I had to

2   step out.

3   But, I do agree with the panel, that we need a

4   comprehensive strategy. Right now, there is no strategy.

5   As an element and -- really, just as an element, I do want

6   to talk a little bit more about arming the Kurds. Of

7   course, this is a passion of mine. So, over the past couple

8   of months, I have been advocating for the administration to

9   increase its support to the Kurdish regional government in

10 Iraq to fight ISIS. And I believe that this is a

11 commonsense proposal, considering the Peshmerga's

12 willingness to fight -- they are willing to fight -- in

13 close combat. And it is truly unmatched by any other group

14 in that region in the fight against ISIS.

15   The Kurdish people have been vital in supporting our

16 coalition efforts to defeat ISIS and in providing support to

17 around the 1.6 million displaced persons from Iraq and

18 Syria. And also, for the past quarter century, Iraqi Kurds

19 have proven to be reliable partners by supporting U.S.

20 interests every time that we have sought their assistance.

21 And I have spoken with many of the men that have served up

22 in that region, and they always state what great allies the

23 Kurds have been to them in our fight. So, they are proven

24 to be great allies of ours.

25   Earlier this week, former CIA and NSA Director, General

1   Michael Hayden, once again spoke for the need to increase

2   U.S. support to the Kurds in the fight against ISIS. And,

3   on Tuesday, General Hayden said, "I would double down on the

4   Kurds. Their military has the virtue of showing up when it

5   comes to a fight, and they've been our friends in the area

6   for decades."

7   I would tend to agree with him. But, I would love to

8   ask each of you to please explain that, if you do agree with

9   General Hayden's assessment or if you disagree, and maybe

10   why. So, please, to the panel -- General Keane, if we might

11   start with you.

12   Thank you.

13   General Keane: Yes, certainly I agree with that. The

14   problem we have is -- and they've told you, and they've told

15   others, that they're not getting the kinds of arms that they

16   need, the quantity of those arms are not there. We're

17   passing that through the Iraqi government. We probably

18   should have continued the covert problem -- program we did

19   have with -- passing it through the Central Intelligence

20   Agency, and we probably would have had them armed by now if

21   we did it robustly. But, they also need advisors. Because,

22   when they're fighting, they need coordination with airpower

23   to make their ground operations that much more effective.

24   And I would say this. As good as the Kurds are, they

25   have, also, a limited interest in what they're willing to

1   fight for inside Iraq. And they certainly are not going to

2   participate in reclaiming Anbar Province and other parts of

3   Iraq. So, yes, we have to do what we should for the Kurds,

4   but we also need to recognize that a lot more needs to be

5   done with others, as well.

6   And I'll leave it to my colleagues, here, who have more

7   information than I do.

8   Senator Ernst: Right. Thank you.

9   Dr. Kagan.

10   Dr. Kagan: Thank you, Senator.

11   I agree with General Keane, especially about the last

12 point. We certainly should help the Kurds defend Kurdistan.

13 There's no question about that. And we could be doing more

14 than we are. But, the Kurds cannot retake Arab Iraq for --

15 on behalf of the Arabs. And I think, in -- although the

16 Kurds are not remotely -- I don't want to put the Kurds in

17 the category of Shi'a militias, because they absolutely are

18 not, and they don't behave that way. Nevertheless, I think

19 if you saw large Kurdish forces in Mosul for a long period

20 of time, you would find that you would have an ethnic war on

21 your hands that would not be in our interest and would make

22 room for ISIS or its successor to come in. So, I don't

23 think the Kurds could actually do what we need them to do,

24 even if they wanted to.

25   I would only add that, although I agree that we should

1   -- that the Kurds have been very reliable allies, fighting

2   on the ground against our common enemies, they have been

3   less than helpful in Baghdad, repeatedly, and they still are

4   being somewhat less than helpful than they might be, on a

5   number of issues, including demands for oil revenues and

6   various other things.

7   I do believe that we should assist them in their

8   defense, but I also think that we should use that assistance

9   as leverage to try to get the Kurds to think a little bit

10   more about the interests of Iraq as a whole, from a

11   political standpoint, than they sometimes do.

12   Senator Ernst: Thank you.

13   Colonel Harvey.

14   Colonel Harvey: I agree with what has already been

15   said on this issue. I would add that the Sunni Arab

16   communities along the green line, the fault lines, are

17   tremendous numbers of friction points there, about

18   territory, about past grievances. So, we would have to be

19   very careful about how we -- how they would be employed.

20   And I think, you know, that's about making sure that there

21   are red lines about how far they could go in coordination,

22   where they are willing to fight along the frontiers where

23   the Islamic State controls land. We do not want to further

24   polarize these communities more than they are already. But,

25   arming them effectively and developing a mechanism to

1 accommodate Baghdad's interest about knowing what's being

2 delivered, but making sure that it gets delivered -- we have

3 to figure a way to just get that done and coordinate that,

4 but deliver those weapons that are going to be very

5 important to the defense of those Kurdish lands.

6   Senator Ernst: Thank you.

7   Mr. Katulis: Very quickly, Senator, three points.

8   First, in principle, I think it's an idea worth --

9 worthy of consideration. The first point, though -- in my

10 recent visits to Kurdistan, the divisions that still exist

11 inside of the Kurdish Peshmerga, and some of the political

12 divisions -- the KDP and the PUK having separate lines of

13 control -- to actually implement that effectively, they'll

14 need to deal with those divisions.

15   The second is that you have actors in the region,

16 including us, beyond us, regional actors who have offered

17 some of this support. And sometimes it's been blocked by

18 Baghdad, itself. There are sensitivities to even the

19 proposal, because it leads to questions of, "Oh, are you

20 trying to break up Iraq?" And I think we need to be careful

21 in the presentation of that.

22   Which leads to a third point relevant to Iraq, to

23 Syria, to the region more broadly. The more that the United

24 States or other actors within the region invest in

25 subnational actors or nonstate actors for the benefit of

1   trying to defeat terrorist organizations like ISIS, there's

2   advantages to that, because oftentimes they're more capable,

3   as we've seen with the Kurdish Peshmerga. There's a

4   potential long-term disadvantage to it, in that the

5   fragmentation of states, the -- could accelerate if -- if

6   we're working in the short term to defeat a threat and to

7   deal with a counterterrorism issue, but the building blocks

8   that we're putting into place actually then contribute to

9   what I've seen, especially in Syria -- and again, I'm not

10   arguing against it; it's just the potential downside risk in

11   the long term, the notion that we could further

12   inadvertently accelerate the fragmentation of these state

13   entities.

14   Senator Ernst: Well, thank you. I appreciate that

15   very much. And the idea, I believe, and where I am coming

16   from, is that we simply have no strategy in that region, not

17   one that has been communicated clearly to any of us. So, I

18   think establishing at least a safe zone -- I do agree that

19   the Peshmerga -- their interest is only in Kurdistan, it is

20   not moving out into the rest of Iraq. I understand that.

21   But, at least establishing a safe zone within Iraq that is

22   free of ISIS is a step in the right direction. I think we

23   need to think about that, we need to pursue that.

24   But, any thoughts on where -- just your idea of where

25   the administration needs to go, at this point? I still see

1 some reluctance coming from the administration on admitting

2 that ISIS continues to expand, not just within Iraq, but

3 also globally. I -- any thoughts on what we need to do or

4 how we can work with the administration on developing a

5 strategy, one that will work?

6   Yes, please.

7   Mr. Katulis: I would stress, again, where I focus on,

8 which is the regional aspects. I think what the U.S. can do

9 more of -- my colleagues have talked about, militarily and

10 other things -- it's beyond my expertise. The fact that the

11 anti-ISIL coalition has five working groups -- a military

12 one, one on countering violent extremism, on

13 counterterrorism funding, on foreign fighters and

14 stabilization -- I would suggest that those mechanisms are a

15 great template, but also that they've not been used

16 effectively.

17   And, going back to the point I was trying to make, in

18 the region, that I think it's wise to actually try to

19 channel the resources and the efforts of others to much more

20 constructive ends. We often debate about what we do. And I

21 think we need to do more. That's clear. And I think we

22 need to lead. But, using these mechanisms in the anti-ISIL

23 coalition more effectively, having more followup on things

24 like -- we often think it's soft, but it's not -- the

25 countering-violent-extremism efforts, it's not sufficient to

1   me to have a 1- or 2-day conference without any clear,

2   precise followups. And I -- I mean, I think they're talking

3   about it, but we need to have great clarity to our regional

4   partners in knowing -- those in the coalition -- of, "Okay,

5   this is what we're going to do." In the way that General

6   Keane and Derek and Dr. Harvey have talked about -- Dr.

7   Kagan have talked about -- in the military steps, we also

8   need a campaign that is multifaceted on those regards, that,

9   again, nests at its core what we do, but in partnership with

10 others.

11   Senator Ernst: Thank you.

12   Yes, sir.

13   Colonel Harvey: I think that, given the President's

14 strategy and the lines of operation that they have had, I

15 don't think those were ever given an opportunity to succeed,

16 because, even though I thought that they were insufficient

17 to the task last summer, in September, when he declared

18 them, they have not been adequately resourced, organized, or

19 executed, to date. And again, as I said in my opening

20 statement, that's here in Washington, D.C., at the

21 interagency level, as well as in theater.

22   So, if we're not going to be determined to achieve

23 results and have leadership that drives the interagency and

24 makes this a matter of urgency and criticality to the United

25 States, then we're not going to get where we need to go.

1   So, you need to, first, be determined to achieve results.

2   Two, we need to think about some core objectives here.

3   One, we can fight ISIS and still contain Iran and seek to

4   achieve an independent Iraq that is not a client of Tehran.

5   In order to do that, we need to support Sunni Arab

6   engagement and political inclusion. Without adequate force

7   structure on the ground, and commitment, you cannot get out

8   there and engage with the Sunni Arabs, you can't move around

9   the battlespace. And they won't believe you're serious

10   unless you put enough skin in the game.

11   And to do that, we're going to need, in my judgment,

12   about 15,000 or more enhancement of U.S. force structure in

13   theater. And to go to what General Keane said, we need

14   probably two brigades, we need aviation -- a mixed aviation

15   brigade, you need some artillery, you need enhanced direct-

16   action SOF operational capabilities to -- for direct action.

17   Direct action brings you the intelligence, which you then

18   share and allows you to go after those networks.

19   The Islamic State has not been stressed across its

20   large perimeter that it has, from the Syrian border up along

21   the Kurdish green line. They have tremendous

22   vulnerabilities. But, they have had the initiative, because

23   they have not been pressed along that large frontal area

24   that they have.

25   Senator Ernst: Sir, so, just to be clear, you are

1   stating that you believe 15,000 additional troops and

2   aviation assets to directly engage ISIS as a combat --

3   Colonel Harvey: No, I want them to be there to provide

4   the enablers, support for the Iraqi Security Forces for

5   direct action of the Special Operations Forces for indirect

6   fires, advisors embedded with Iraqi Security Forces or

7   Ministry of Interior elements, in a way that gets us on the

8   ground, can bring in our capabilities. I'm not advising

9   that we put troops on the ground in combat outposts in

10   Ramadi, clearing streets, you know, and communities and

11   neighborhoods in a direct-action way. But, we need to be

12   out there enabling and providing support and protection for

13   Sunni Arab tribal militias, helping them grow and develop,

14   and then that gives us influence that can reach into the

15   political domain in the -- these provinces, but also in

16   Baghdad. It's hard to have influence if you don't have skin

17   in the game.

18   Senator Ernst: I would agree with that. I would also

19   state, though, that anytime you do engage more of those

20   types of troops on the ground, you may say that it is a

21   train-and-assist mission, and that may be heavier on the

22   assist mission, but we are engaging in combat at that point.

23   I don't think there's any way that you avoid that. And I

24   don't want to mislead the American people, because certainly

25   there is danger anytime that we put troops on the ground.

1   So, I'm not saying I would support, or not support, that

2   measure, but I do believe that you are correct, sir, in that

3   we do need to engage if we expect others to engage. We know

4   that the airstrikes are not doing it. So, thank you for

5   that perspective.

6   Dr. Kagan: Senator, I want to second what Derek said,

7   and agree with him about the need to deploy forces. I agree

8   with you, and I know that Derek also does, that it's -- the

9   purpose of talking about train, advise, and assist, in this

10   context, is not to imply that American troops are not going

11   to be in combat. Of course they are, if we're doing our

12   job. But, I think the point that Derek was trying to make,

13   which is very important, is that we're not anticipating

14   putting American brigades in Ramadi and having them clear,

15   house to house, the way we have done previously.

16   Senator Ernst: Thank you.

17   Dr. Kagan: That's not what we're looking at.

18   I have to say, we, as a Nation, are defeated as long as

19   we do not have the will to fight this war. And I would

20   assess right now, we seem to be showing that we do not have

21   the will to fight this war. And until and unless the --

22   beginning with the President, there is a demonstration that

23   we have the will to fight, we are going to lose this war.

24   And so, what Congress has to do, what we all have to do, is

25   find any way that we can to persuade the President to own

1   this fight, to recognize that it's a war, to recognize that

2   we must win, and to help develop the will among the American

3   people to fight this.

4   Senator Ernst: Thank you very much.

5   General Keane: The thing -- the only thing I would add

6   is that you do have to look at this strategically. When you

7   think -- the World Trade Center in '93 was the introduction

8   of radical Islam directly against the United States, not

9   using proxies that the Iranians did since 1980. And that

10 was followed by Embassy bombings in Africa, the U.S.S. Cole,

11 and 9/11. And, to date, we've gone through three

12 administrations, and we've never developed a comprehensive

13 strategy to deal with it. We're sitting here today without

14 one, despite all of that killing, despite all of the

15 aggressiveness and assertiveness that this enemy has showed.

16 We have always looked at this narrowly. And it's tragic

17 that we do. And we're more sophisticated than that.

18   Yes, the solution is right in front of us. When you

19 look at this map -- look at -- this is just ISIS. If I put

20 al-Qaeda on the map, it would be worse. This is a regional

21 and global problem that can only be solved by those

22 countries who are being affected by this, either directly or

23 indirectly. This is not about the United States dealing

24 with all of this; this is about the United States, when

25 we're hosting a conference, like we just did, as opposed to

1   shaking hands and slapping everybody on the back, which we
2   did, we should have hosted a conference that came out with a
3   strategy on what to do with this, plans on what to do with
4   this. What is the level of contribution that's going to
5   deal with this? We don't develop that strategy. Together,
6   we can design a comprehensive strategy that does undermine
7   the ideology, that does take their finances away, and that
8   does meet this threat, militarily, where it needs to be met.
9   We cannot do this by ourselves. We have no
10 comprehensive strategies to deal with radical Islam, to
11 include ISIS. We have no strategy in the region to deal
12 with the morphing of radical Islam, as defined by ISIS and
13 al-Qaeda. And we certainly -- as we've all been saying, we
14 have no strategy immediately to deal -- effective strategy
15 to deal with this issue in Iraq and Syria.
16   So, I agree with you, that is the start point that we
17 should have to deal with this problem. And then you start
18 to put underneath that those things that make sense. And
19 we've got to bring our allies into this in a very cohesive
20 way. Listen, they've -- we have their attention. The
21 Iranians are forcing their attention, ISIS is forcing their
22 attention, and the spread of al-Qaeda. We have to help them
23 organize to do this effort, and bring the means to deal with
24 that. And not all of that is kinetic. And certainly most
25 of it is not United States military power.

1   Senator Ernst: Yes. Thank you very much.

2   And, General Keane, you brought up Iranian influences.

3   And since I have come into the Senate, I have been very,

4   very concerned about the Iranian influence with the Shi'a

5   militia. And here we have the Shi'a militia pushing back

6   against ISIS. And I would love to hear a little bit more

7   about that Iranian influence with the Shi'a militia. Where

8   do we go from here? Assuming that we do take care of ISIS,

9   the Shi'a are controlling areas, but their intent, I think,

10 could easily turn against American influences, American

11 soldiers that might be on the ground there. So, as we look

12 at arming the Shi'a militia, if we talk about that, engaging

13 with them, just remembering that they are being influenced

14 heavily by the Iranians, and -- what would your thoughts be

15 on that?

16   Dr. Kagan: Senator, I'd like to say I don't think the

17 Shi'a -- the Iraqi Shi'a are the problem. And there are

18 elements in the Popular Mobilization Forces and so forth

19 that I think are not pro-Iranian and do not desire to be

20 governed by Iran. We've seen this repeatedly. And, of

21 course, this is the view of Grand Ayatollah Sistani and his

22 -- the people who follow him, is that Iraq is an Arab

23 country, it's not a Persian country, and they don't want to

24 be dominated by Persians.

25   However, the most effective Shi'a militia forces are

1   part of the Iranian military, de facto. The Badr Corps, run

2   by Hadi al-Amiri, reports to Qassem Suleimani, the commander

3   of the Quds Force. Kata'ib Hezbollah, run by Muhandis,

4   reports to Qassem Suleimani, commander of the Quds Force.

5   And we have seen this repeatedly. So, we have -- it's not a

6   Shi'a problem. It is a specific problem of Iranian --

7   they're no longer even really proxies. They're now really

8   extensions of the Iranian irregular military forces, and

9   those are the elements that are now leading the charge into

10   Ramadi, which is unacceptable.

11   They also helped to get us off track by launching the

12   attack on Tikrit on their own, spontaneously, which then

13   failed, and we had to bail them out, which was an enormous

14   positive turning point for us, because it demonstrated the

15   limitations of the ability of those Iranian-controlled Iraqi

16   militias to take this fight to the enemy. We have just not

17   only undone that benefit that we gained from that, but moved

18   many steps back. And if, in fact, these groups are

19   successful in retaking even part of Ramadi, when the troops

20   that we backed failed, it will demonstrate the viability of

21   these elements within Iraq in a catastrophic way that will

22   undermine Prime -- any independence Prime Minister Abadi

23   might have, any independence the ISF might have, and be a

24   significant extension of Iranian military power, not just

25   political influence, in the region.

1   Senator Ernst: Thank you.

2   Chairman McCain: I'd just --

3   Senator Ernst: Yes, I -- my time is way over, Senator.

4   Chairman McCain: I was going to say, I'm glad you were

5 able to have --

6   Senator Ernst: I could go all day.

7   Chairman McCain: -- this encounter. I hope you'll

8 have them over to your house for dinner.

9   Senator Ernst: I would love that.

10   Thank you very much, gentlemen.

11   Chairman McCain: Before I turn to Senator Kaine -- and

12 I apologize for this disjointedness of the votes on the

13 floor -- I -- maybe, General Keane and Colonel Harvey,

14 particularly you two, can respond to this. I don't know if

15 there's a real logical argument to the -- that would counter

16 what has been said here today, as far as the assessment of

17 the overall situation is concerned, because I think the

18 facts on the ground are -- would indicate that there's

19 strong support for the argument or the position that you

20 have stated. But yet, we have members of the military, who

21 many years of experience, who have fought in Iraq and

22 Afghanistan, and yet, as military spokesmen, or even

23 military leaders, make statements that are totally divorced,

24 if not -- I won't say "reality," but certainly is directly

25 counter to the testimony that you have given here today. I

1   do not understand it.

2   Maybe, Colonel Harvey, could I begin with you?

3   Colonel Harvey: Sir, what I find is, quite often our

4   commanders and leaders are misreading the operational

5   environment that they're dealing with. They don't

6   understand the enemy well enough. And part of the problem

7   there is, the intelligence that they get is reporting of

8   information, it's not being put in context in a very

9   insightful and deep way to understand how they are

10   organized, how they really think, tactically, operationally,

11   and strategically. It's reporting history rather than

12   thinking about who they really are and what the enemy's

13   doing.

14   Chairman McCain: Does that account for statements

15   like, "We're winning"?

16   Colonel Harvey: Because they're looking at the wrong

17   metrics. As I said in my opening statement, sir, you know,

18   in order to get the context, you really need to deep -- have

19   the deep dives and focus in on this, and quit looking at

20   this on a day-to-day basis. And you have to have an

21   operational construct. You have to understand who the enemy

22   is and how they're going to win. You -- and probably we

23   need better alternative analysis about this, and be truthful

24   to ourselves about how we're doing in our lines of

25   operation.

1   Chairman McCain: So, this is an argument for Team B.

2   Colonel Harvey: In part, yes, sir. We had group-think

3   before, in 2005 and 2006. In May have 2006, we were being

4   told that everything's on track --

5   Chairman McCain: I --

6   Colonel Harvey: -- we're doing fine.

7   Chairman McCain: I remember it well.

8   Colonel Harvey: Yes, sir.

9   They get built-in assumptions and they're focused in

10   what their mission set is. Where is the order to actually

11   impose our will and defeat the enemy? How are we going to

12   align our force structure and all of our national

13   capabilities, in partnership with allies and folks on the

14   ground that we can count on, to build momentum, to impose

15   our will, to establish security? We don't think in those

16   terms anymore. We talk about management rather than

17   breaking the will of the enemy.

18   Chairman McCain: General Keane.

19   General Keane: Yes, sir. I mean, it -- I share your

20   frustration. I know we all share it. We talk about it

21   among ourselves quite a bit. We just had a spokesperson,

22   last week -- I think that's probably what you're referring

23   to -- who made a report, you know, to the American people at

24   large, that we, in fact, were succeeding against ISIS, that

25   we're pushing back against them, and that they're only

1   capable of conducting small attacks against us.

2   Chairman McCain: Right --

3   General Keane: That hasn't --

4   Chairman McCain: -- before Ramadi fell.

5   General Keane: That hasn't been true since we started,

6   and certainly isn't true now. So, one, how do we -- this

7   committee members, when I provided testimony in 2006 and we

8   were pushing against the narrative at that time by senior

9   generals and Secretaries of Defense, et cetera, we were

10   asked the same question. How could that be? How could

11   capable people, well-intentioned, be so wrong, in general

12   sense, is the issue. And I think once we make up our minds

13   that we're going to do something inside this military

14   culture, we drive towards it. And we have a tendency, to a

15   fault, to see those indices that contribute to what that

16   mission success is, and to disregard -- not wholly, but to

17   minimize those things that are really pushing against it.

18   That's inside our culture.

19   How do you fix that? One way, and one way only:

20   competent leadership fixes that. You don't permit that to

21   happen, because you are driving honest, tough, deep-dive

22   assessments of what's taking place, "This is what we're

23   trying to do. These are the four things we said we were

24   going to do. How are we doing that?"

25   How could you ever come to the conclusion that ISIS is

1   losing if it enjoys freedom of maneuver, a principle of

2   warfare, and it can attack, at will, any place of its

3   choosing at any time of its choosing? If a force has that

4   capability to do that, and gets results as a -- as a

5   manifestation of that, then that force, in fact, by

6   definition, is winning.

7   And so, the leader should say to those subordinates

8   below him, say, "What are you talking about? You're -- what

9   you're telling me, none of that makes any sense. This is

10   what this force is doing. This is what they're capable of.

11   We have got this wrong, and how are we going to fix it?"

12   That is about competent leadership.

13   Chairman McCain: Senator Kaine.

14   Senator Kaine: Thank you, Mr. Chair.

15   And I'm jealous of my colleague's 13 minutes, and I

16   hope my other colleagues don't come back, and then I may try

17   your patience and go over time.

18   Dr. Kagan, you said something that I wrote down, just

19   like a bolt of lightning, "We should not just be

20   spectators." You were going through the atrocities that

21   ISIL is committing, and who they are, and how dangerous they

22   are, "We should not just be spectators." We are spectators.

23   Congress -- Congress has been a spectator. Since August 8,

24   we've been a spectator.

25   Absent the one vote, in September, that we took to arm

1   Syrian moderates, there is no evidence that Congress is

2   concerned at all about ISIL. None. Our allies have no

3   evidence that Congress is concerned -- as an institution;

4   I'm not talking about individuals -- our allies have no

5   evidence that Congress is concerned about ISIL. ISIL has no

6   evidence that Congress is concerned about ISIL. But, most

7   tragically, the thousands of people -- U.S. men and women in

8   service who are deployed and fighting this battle every day,

9   they have no evidence that Congress is concerned about ISIL,

10 in the least.

11   We've been at war since August the 8th. Everybody

12 calls it a war. The President calls it a war. Within 2

13 weeks, the Article 2 mission to defend the Embassy and the

14 Consulate in Arbil were pretty safe. And he said, "We've

15 got to go on the offense against ISIL." And Presidents

16 since Jefferson have basically said that was the dividing

17 line between an Article 2 power of the Commander in Chief

18 and an Article 1 power, where Congress has got to declare

19 war or authorize military action.

20   But, now, for 9 and a half months, we have failed to do

21 what is our fundamental job, what only we are supposed to do

22 -- there's not been a declaration of war, there's not been

23 an authorization for use of military force, there's been no

24 House committee action, there's been no House floor debate

25 or vote. There was one committee vote, in the Senate

1   Foreign Relations Committee in December, but there's been no

2   meaningful floor debate and no meaningful Senate floor

3   action.

4   How strange it is. We're in a Congress that loves to

5   punch this President as an imperial President, and threaten

6   lawsuits against him when he does stuff without

7   congressional approval. In the most solemn responsibility

8   under Article 1 that Congress has, we have been silent, when

9   we've got all these people overseas who are risking their

10   lives every day, we have been silent. It's Congress that's

11   the spectators. We've got opinions. You know, we'd call

12   the play differently. But, we're spectators when we ought

13   to be decisionmakers.

14   This is now a war, into the 10th month, without a clear

15   legal basis. I call it extralegal or even illegal. The

16   President, himself, has, in his own words, acknowledged that

17   he's gone past the Article 2 power of imminent defense. The

18   claim that the 2001 or 2002 authorizations cover an

19   organization that didn't form til 2 years after 9/11, that

20   doesn't make any sense. It doesn't make any sense

21   whatsoever.

22   And yet, Congress has come up with one excuse after

23   another to avoid taking action. The first excuse was this.

24   The leaders -- both parties, both houses -- the four

25   leaders went to the White House in June and said, "Do not

1 make us take action on this war. You do what you want. Do

2 not make us take action in Congress before the midterm

3 elections." And Congress adjourned, with an ongoing war, 6

4 weeks before a midterm election. The earliest adjournment

5 since 1960 before a midterm election with an ongoing war,

6 and we haven't done anything about it.

7   After the midterm election, then it was, "Well, but now

8 the Senate's going to change hands, so we shouldn't do

9 anything gas a lameduck Senate, because there will be a new

10 Senate." So, we waited til January.

11   Then we came in, and a lot of folks said, "Well, you

12 know, we shouldn't do our Article 1 job, because the

13 President hasn't sent us a draft authorization." I harshly

14 criticize the administration for not sending in a draft

15 authorization over right when they started this legal

16 action. But, the fact that they didn't doesn't excuse

17 Congress for not doing the job we're supposed to do.

18   And now there's been an authorization pending before

19 Congress since the 17th of February, more than 3 months, and

20 we still haven't done anything. And I don't know what the

21 excuse is now.

22   I think you can only conclude that we don't want to

23 take it up because we're either indifferent to this threat

24 -- and I don't think that's true. I think the real reason

25 is, we don't have the backbone to take it up and do the job

1   that Congress is supposed to do. And what that means is,

2   while we're not doing our job, there are others who are

3   doing their job. We deployed thousands into the theater of

4   battle, two folks who are pilots, off the deck of the

5   Theodore Roosevelt, which was -- which is home-ported in

6   Virginia, crashed a plane on takeoff the other day. We're

7   deploying thousands, and they're risking their lives. We

8   have had deaths of American servicemen in connection with

9   Operation Inherent Resolve. We had -- have had deaths of

10   American civilians who were held hostage. ISIL didn't start

11   executing American hostages until after we started bombing

12   them on the 8th of August. So, we've had American deaths as

13   a result of this war. We still haven't done anything.

14   We've had over 3,000 airstrikes that the U.S. has -- and we

15   still haven't done anything. And now the costs passed the

16   $2 billion mark in April, and we still haven't done

17   anything.

18   It's just -- I never would have contemplated, before I

19   came to this body, that there would be a situation in which

20   Congress would tolerate an ongoing war and just stand back

21   and say, "Well, I guess the President can just do whatever

22   the President wants to do." It's just not supposed to be

23   that way.

24   And one of the reasons I'm glad that the Chair called

25   this committee today, as I'm hoping that the challenging

1 events of last weekend -- not only the fall of Ramadi, but

2 if you go into the details of that Special Forces operation

3 in Syria -- very, very serious. We were lucky that we

4 didn't lose U.S. lives in that operation. It was very well

5 done. But, this is complicated and detailed, and it's going

6 to go on for a very long time. And I just wonder how much

7 longer Congress is going to just be a spectator.

8 I mean, we can criticize the White House and the

9 administration strategy -- and I'm going to, and we ought to

10 keep doing it if we don't like it -- but, we really haven't

11 earned the right -- we haven't earned the right to be

12 critics as long as we stand back and don't do the one thing

13 that Congress is supposed to do.

14 Thank you, Mr. Chair.

15 Chairman McCain: I know there's a question in there

16 somewhere.

17 Senator Graham.

18 Senator Graham: Well, thank you.

19 Here's my question. Does the current strategy in Iraq

20 and Syria have any chance to succeed?

21 General Keane: Well, Senator, that's really been the

22 basis of our testimony. And --

23 Senator Graham: Well, I didn't hear it, so just --

24 General Keane: I know.

25 Senator Graham: -- say no.

1   General Keane: We'll gladly say it again.

2   Senator Graham: Yeah, say it again.

3   General Keane: And respect you asking the question,

4 quite frankly. The answer is no. It's --

5   Senator Graham: Does everybody agree the answer is no?

6 Does everybody agree that, in the current configuration,

7 that the problems in Iraq and Syria present a direct threat

8 to the homeland?

9   General Keane: Yes.

10   Dr. Kagan: Yes.

11   Colonel Harvey: Yes.

12   Senator Graham: I had a conversation with the CIA

13 Director, yesterday, who echoed that sentiment. So, the

14 average American needs to understand that failure in Iraq

15 and Syria is putting the homeland at risk because so many

16 foreign fighters are flowing in, and they have the ability,

17 potentially, to hit us here at home. Is that all correct?

18   General Keane: Yes.

19   Senator Graham: And I think, General Keane, you've

20 described this strategy as not enough. Is that correct?

21   General Keane: Yeah. Absolutely. It's far from it.

22 And we all, collectively, laid out some details to support

23 that.

24   Senator Graham: Do you see any way to defeat ISIL in

25 Syria without a substantial Arab army involved?

1   General Keane: I don't know how you get there. I

2   mean, obviously, if we deployed tens of thousands of troops,

3   ourselves, we could defeat ISIS in Syria. I don't think

4   anybody here would recommend such an event. I think the

5   people who have vested interests there should be involved,

6   and I think they would get involved. I mean, you know that

7   they've said as much, but we have to do something to change

8   the momentum of the Assad regime.

9   Senator Graham: Dr. Kagan, is it fair to say that no

10   Arab army is going into Syria unless part of the -- one of

11   the objectives is to take Assad down?

12   Dr. Kagan: Absolutely, Senator. That's going to be a

13   precondition for --

14   Senator Graham: Because they're not going to just

15   fight ISIL and leave Assad in power, therefore giving the

16   place to Syria. Is that correct?

17   Dr. Kagan: On the contrary, sir.

18   Senator Graham: I mean, to Iran.

19   Dr. Kagan: On the contrary, sir. What we're seeing, I

20   think, is increasing levels of support of various varieties

21   to Jabhat al-Nusra as an alternative to the --

22   Senator Graham: So, I want people to understand that

23   our strategy is to empower a radical Islamic Sunni group to

24   fight Assad rather than having an army on the ground that --

25   made up of allies. Is that fairly accurate?

1   We're choosing to work with terrorists --

2   Dr. Kagan: I think --

3   Senator Graham: -- or somebody's -- the Arabs are

4   choosing to work with terrorists, because there's a vacuum

5   created by us.

6   Dr. Kagan: I think some people are choosing to work

7   with terrorists because of the vacuum that we have created.

8   I don't think that's the intent of our policy.

9   Senator Graham: No, but that's the effect of the

10 policy.

11   Dr. Kagan: I believe it is, yes, sir.

12   Senator Graham: So, we find ourselves where our allies

13 in the region are supporting a terrorist group as a last-

14 resort proposition because America is AWOL.

15   Colonel Harvey, at the end of the day, do you see a

16 scenario of dislodging ISIL, taking Assad out, that doesn't

17 require a sustained commitment by the world to put Syria

18 back together?

19   Colonel Harvey: No, I do not see.

20   Senator Graham: We're talking years, and billions of

21 dollars.

22   Colonel Harvey: I believe so, sir, yes.

23   Senator Graham: All right. Sir, I don't want to

24 butcher your last name. If this war keeps going on the way

25 it is a year from now, do you worry about Jordan and Lebanon

1 being affected?

2   Mr. Katulis: I do, and especially Jordan, a country

3 I've lived in and studied as a Fulbright scholar. We are

4 doing important things to help strengthen that government,

5 but it is feeling the force of not only the --

6   Senator Graham: If we lost the King of Jordan, we'd be

7 losing one of the most trustworthy allies in the region. Is

8 that correct?

9   Mr. Katulis: Correct.

10   Senator Graham: I was told yesterday that there are

11 more Syrian children in elementary school in Lebanon than

12 Lebanese children. Does that surprise anybody?

13   Mr. Katulis: It doesn't surprise me, but it should

14 shock all of us.

15   Senator Graham: Well, it should shock everybody. I've

16 just made a statement that there are more kids in elementary

17 school in Lebanon from Syria than Lebanese kids. So, if

18 this war continues in its current fashion, it will create

19 unending chaos in the Mideast that will change the map for

20 generations to come. Do you all agree with that?

21   Mr. Katulis: Yes.

22   General Keane: Yes.

23   Senator Graham: And there is no way to get Iraq right

24 until you deal with Syria in a responsible manner. Is that

25 correct?

1   General Keane: That is correct.

2   Colonel Harvey: Correct.

3   Senator Graham: And Iran is all in when it comes to

4   Syria. Assad wouldn't last 15 minutes without Iran's help.

5   Do you agree?

6   Colonel Harvey: It's been critical to sustaining the

7   Assad regime. They don't --

8   Senator Graham: Do you agree that, if we gave

9   Iranians, say, $50 billion as a signing bonus for their

10   nuclear program, it's highly likely that some of that money

11   would go to Assad?

12   General Keane: And to the rest of his proxies that are

13   seeking domination of the Middle East.

14   Senator Graham: Have you seen anything to suggest the

15   Iranians are changing their behavior for the better when it

16   comes to the region?

17   Dr. Kagan: On the contrary, sir. They're becoming

18   more aggressive in many facets.

19   Senator Graham: Would you say they're the most

20   aggressive they've been in modern times?

21   Dr. Kagan: Yes, sir.

22   General Keane: Yes.

23   Senator Graham: Would you say that the Iranians are

24   directly responsible for topping -- toppling a pro-American

25   government in Yemen by supporting the Houthis?

1   General Keane: They contributed to it, for sure.

2   Senator Graham: Would you agree with me that, now that

3   we've lost our eyes and ears in Yemen, al-Qaeda in the

4   Arabian Peninsula is growing as a threat to the homeland?

5   Colonel Harvey: Yes.

6   Dr. Kagan: Not only that, but ISIS is also gaining

7   position in Yemen.

8   Senator Graham: Do you agree with me that Syria is now

9   a perfect forum to launch an attack from the United States

10   because there are so many foreign fighters with Western

11   passports?

12   Colonel Harvey: Yes.

13   Senator Graham: Do you agree with me that the Shi'a

14   militia on the ground in Iraq are controlled by the

15   Iranians?

16   Colonel Harvey: Yes.

17   Senator Graham: Do you agree with me that we're doing

18   permanent damage to the ability of Iraq to reconstruct if we

19   allow the Shi'a militia to continue to have dominance on the

20   battlefield?

21   General Keane: Yes.

22   Colonel Harvey: Yes.

23   Senator Graham: Do you see any good thing coming from

24   this strategy being continued?

25   General Keane: No.

        1   Colonel Harvey: No, sir.

        2   General Keane: It's destined to fail.

        3   Senator Graham: And there is a better way. We just

        4   have to choose that way.

        5   Colonel Harvey: Correct, sir.

        6   General Keane: Correct.

        7   Senator Graham: There is a better way. Do you all

        8   agree?

        9   Colonel Harvey: Yes, sir.

       10   General Keane: Yes, sir.

       11   Senator Graham: Thank you.

       12   Chairman McCain: Any more --

       13   Senator Cruz.

       14   Senator Cruz: Thank you, Mr. Chairman.

       15   Gentlemen, thank you very much for being here. Thank

       16   you for your service and your leadership.

       17   I'd like to ask the panel, first, for your assessment

       18   of the current level of success we are seeing in the

       19   military campaign against ISIS.

       20   Dr. Kagan: It is failing, Senator. That's our -- I

       21   think our assessment, generally, across the board, is that

       22   it is failing in Iraq, it is failing in Syria, and it is

       23   failing across the board in the region.

       24   Senator Cruz: And why is it failing?

       25   Dr. Kagan: In my view, it was ill-conceived to begin

1   with, because it focused exclusively on Iraq. It was badly

2   under-resourced, and excessive restraints and constraints

3   have been put on the limited resources that we were willing

4   to deploy.

5   Senator Cruz: Could you please elaborate on the

6   excessive constraints that have been placed on our military?

7   Dr. Kagan: Yes, sir.

8   We have forces in theater that could have made a

9   significant difference, I believe, in the fight for Ramadi,

10   had they been allowed to embed at lower levels, had they

11   been allowed to perform functions of forward air controllers

12   and bring in precision air support, had the -- some of the

13   rotary-wing aviation that we have in theater been used in

14   direct support of that fight, had the forces that we have in

15   theater been able to go out to the tribes and reach out to

16   them directly rather than relying on the tribes to come to

17   them. There were a number of things that even this limited

18   force could have done, I think, that would have made a

19   difference. But, the force was probably too limited to be

20   decisive, in any event.

21   General Keane: Yeah. Now, just to add on to that, I

22   mean -- you know, the military -- these other components to

23   the President's strategy, as you know -- and there's huge

24   problems with them, as well -- but the military component is

25   clearly under-resourced. There's not enough trainers,

1   there's not enough advisors. And the role of the advisors

2   is fundamentally flawed, itself. The advisors have to be

3   down where the units are doing the fighting, at least at the

4   battalion level. What reason is that? Because they help

5   them plan, they help them execute, they contribute to their

6   success, they have the capability to call in airstrikes,

7   they have the capability to use drones in support of those

8   ground forces to help acquire intelligence for them, and

9   they can use attack helicopters, as well.

10   And therefore, the airstrikes that we currently have,

11   which are excellent in taking out command and control, other

12   infrastructure, logistic infrastructures, depots --

13   essentially, facilities -- they get -- it starts to fall off

14   very rapidly when you're dealing with mobile targets. And

15   then, Senator, the overwhelming amount of combat that takes

16   place, to use military terms, is close combat in urban

17   centers that are populated and where we get -- we, our

18   forces, Iraqi forces -- get very close to the enemy. To be

19   able to do that, you have to guide the bombs from that

20   airplane, take control of them. And that's called close air

21   support. That's what we need the forward air controllers

22   for.

23   So, the effectiveness of our airpower is this: 75

24   percent of the missions that are flown come back with their

25   bombs, because they cannot acquire the target or properly

1   identify the target so they have some assurances that

2   they're not going to hit -- hurt somebody with those bombs

3   that we don't want to be hurt. That changes dramatically if

4   we put those forward air controllers on the ground.

5   I'll tell you what. If you're fighting as the fighting

6   took place in Ramadi, and, as that fight unfolded, the

7   scenario was -- they had prepared, for weeks, to get to

8   Ramadi. This was not due to a sandstorm. This is taking

9   out supporting towns, other attacks, diversionary attacks,

10   that led to, finally, an assault using suicide-bombers'

11   vehicles to do that. If that force had antitank weapons,

12   they could have killed those vehicles. If they had Apache

13   helicopters, they could have killed those vehicles. Those

14   vehicles blew up and destroyed almost entire blocks, and

15   destroyed entire units, because the explosives were so heavy

16   on it.

17   After that came the fighting forces, themselves. If --

18   again, if we had close air support, we could easily deal

19   with those fighting forces before they actually closed with

20   the Iraqi military. Apache helicopters, close air support,

21   would have significantly impacted them. And then we have a

22   close fight, and assuming the Iraqi forces could deal with

23   that.

24   But, I would tell you this. Many of those Iraqi forces

25   -- it's not reported -- did fight heroically in Ramadi. And

1   a lot of them fled. But, that resolve gets stiffened very

2   quickly when they watch those suicide bombers get blown up

3   before they get to them, when they watch those units --

4   those caravans coming down the road after them get blown up

5   before they get to them, because we have proper

6   surveillance, we have resources that can deal with that --

7   antitank guided missiles and the like. We start to change

8   the dimension on the battlefield very significantly as a

9   result of providing them with the proper resources.

10   These are the constraints that are out there that are

11   manifesting itself in the behavior of the Iraqi Security

12   Forces. They have their own problems -- leadership,

13   discipline, morale, and competence. I'm not suggesting that

14   they don't. But, there's a lot we could do that could make

15   a difference.

16   Senator Cruz: Let me ask one final question, which is:

17   The administration is currently declining to arm the Kurds.

18   The Peshmerga are fighting ISIS. They are effective

19   fighters. They have been allies of America. In my

20   judgment, the policy of not arming the Kurds makes very

21   little sense. I would be interested in the panel's

22   assessment of, Should we be arming the Kurds? And is the

23   current policy reasonable and effective in defeating ISIS?

24   Dr. Kagan: Sir, we -- I think it's a consensus on the

25   panel that we should be helping the Kurds defend themselves,

1   but that the Kurds will not be able to be effective partners

2   in retaking the portions of Arab Iraq that ISIS now

3   controls, but that certainly we should be helping the Kurds

4   defend themselves, I think.

5   Chairman McCain: Could I point out the -- actually,

6   we're not refusing to arm the Kurds. The problem is, it

7   goes through Baghdad, and the Kurds continue to complain

8   that there is not the kind of facilitation of the delivery

9   of those weapons. But, the Senator's point is, for all

10 practical purposes, I think, correct.

11   Senator King.

12   Senator King: One of the -- a phrase you just used

13 struck a chord with me. It -- there was weeks in

14 preparation for going to Ramadi -- raises the question of

15 intelligence. And, General Keane, would you comment? Do we

16 have adequate intelligence? Do we have any intelligence?

17 And have we become too reliant on signals intelligence and,

18 therefore, don't have human beings giving us information?

19   General Keane: Yeah, I mean, that's a great question.

20 And it's more appropriately put to the military leaders when

21 they come in here, because they have the details of it, and

22 -- but, this much I do know. My sensing, from talking to my

23 sources, is the intelligence function is not robust enough.

24 And it -- yes, we are relying on national intelligence

25 sources and some regional intelligence sources. Some of

1   that is surveillance, some of that is, you know, signals

2   intelligence, as well. But, there's a lot more that we can

3   do to assist them. We use surveillance a lot to assist the

4   use of airpower, because it's not controlled by forward air

5   controllers. We need different kinds of surveillance in

6   there to assist ground forces.

7   When we were fighting in Iraq, and now finishing up in

8   Afghanistan, our maneuver units used different kinds of

9   drones. They've much smaller. They don't stay up,

10   necessarily, as long as the ones that assist the airpower

11   function. And they assist the ground commanders. That kind

12   of capability there, controlled by U.S., would dramatically

13   make a difference for the ground forces that are in the

14   fight, because that would give them the ability to see the

15   preparations the enemy is making, to see the execution

16   before they -- it impacts on them, and, most importantly, to

17   do something about it.

18   I think the entire intelligence function has got to be

19   put under review. We have a tendency to focus on other

20   things that are kinetic --

21   Senator King: Right.

22   General Keane: -- but the intelligence function, in

23   this kind of warfare, is significant, in terms of its

24   enhancing ground forces and air forces to be able to use

25   their capabilities to the fullest.

1   Senator King: And it's unfortunate that we continue to

2 -- we seem to continue to be surprised.

3   Did you --

4   Colonel Harvey: Sir, if I could, on the Ramadi issue,

5 just -- I'm at the University of South Florida, and, you

6 know, we drafted a paper outlining that Ramadi was going to

7 fall, early last week, and we were looking at data that's

8 only available to us through open-source information, but

9 understanding the enemy, their intent, trying to get inside

10 how they're orchestrating the fight. And it's not just

11 about having the intelligence, it's knowing what to do with

12 the information and how to think about it.

13   The warnings were there, the indicators were there. If

14 we could see it, at the University of South Florida, and

15 others here in -- like the Institute for the Study of War, I

16 think, also saw that -- then we shouldn't have been making

17 public statements, midweek, officially saying that Ramadi

18 was not going to fall, that it wasn't really under threat,

19 because that creates another problem of its own, because

20 then you have the collapse, and it looks like there's a real

21 problem in our communication and understanding at the most

22 -- highest levels of our government.

23   Senator King: Well, and also it makes the ISIS look

24 invincible and more powerful, and that's -- helps in their

25 recruiting, and it becomes a self-fulfilling prophecy.

1   You've made a strong case for things like close air

2   support, forward controllers, all of those kinds of things.

3   But, isn't one of the fundamental problems -- we could have

4   all of those assets, but, if the Iraqi Security Forces don't

5   have the will to fight, and if the local population doesn't

6   have the -- any confidence in the government in Baghdad,

7   it's still a very difficult, if not impossible, proposition.

8   Can you give me some thoughts on that?

9   Dr. Kagan: Senator, I agree with the statement that

10   you made. If those two conditions are true, then it's

11   difficult, to impossible. I don't think it's true that the

12   Iraqi forces don't have the will to fight. I think they do

13   have the will to fight. But, I think, as General Keane

14   pointed out and as we've seen repeatedly, will to fight is

15   one thing, belief in your ability to succeed is another

16   critical component to will to fight. And that's one of the

17   things that we have provided, historically, to our allies in

18   Iraq and Afghanistan, and also to NATO allies and various

19   other partners who rely on our overmatching military

20   capabilities just as much as the Iraqis would. We can make

21   it so that the Iraqis don't have to worry about being

22   overrun. That's what we used to do. We are allowing them

23   to be overrun in these circumstances. And that erodes their

24   will to fight, significantly.

25   Your point about the political accommodation is also

1   incredibly important. We absolutely need to have an Iraqi

2   government that is prepared to reach out to Sunni

3   effectively. And we haven't seen that. Unfortunately, the

4   more that we try to subcontract these conflicts to local

5   forces in preference to our own --

6   Senator King: Then you're talking about the --

7   Dr. Kagan: -- you get a --

8   Senator King: -- Shi'a militia.

9   Dr. Kagan: Exactly, sir.

10   Senator King: Which only exacerbates the sectarian

11   conflict, which makes ISIS look good to the Sunni chiefs in

12   Anbar.

13   Dr. Kagan: Or more tolerable, perhaps, than the

14   alternatives.

15   Senator King: Yeah. I don't think they look good to

16   anybody.

17   Dr. Kagan: Yes, sir.

18   Senator King: It's -- but, if they don't have

19   confidence -- I mean, isn't that one of the fundamental

20   problems here, is that ISIS has been swimming in, if not a

21   friendly sea, at least a neutral sea, in terms of the Sunni

22   provinces?

23   Dr. Kagan: I think it's a very fearful sea. And I

24   think that that's -- you know, we shouldn't forget that

25   terrorism works both ways, and these guys are incredibly

1   brutal in dealing with the populations that they control.

2   So, people are going to require a certain amount of

3   assurance that, if they rise up against these guys, that

4   they will win, because it -- the alternative is that they

5   will be completely destroyed as communities.

6   General Keane: You know, the other thing is, the force

7   that we had in Iraq, the Iraqi Security Force that took us

8   -- it took us a while to get them to be effective, to be

9   frank about it. And one of the things that made them very

10   effective during the surge period, where General Petraeus

11   changed the dimension on the battlefield, and he said,

12   "We're not just going to provide them advisors, we're going

13   to ask them to fight side by side with us" -- platoon, side

14   by side; company, side by side; battalion, side by side.

15   That dimension exponentially increased the capability of the

16   force, because they could see what right looked like. They

17   could see it. It was right there. A sergeant could see a

18   U.S. sergeant's performance, how he acted under stress.

19   Soldiers could see it. Other leaders could see their

20   counterparts' performance.

21   So, that force grew rather dramatically, and we were

22   there multiple weeks throughout 2007 and 2008, the three of

23   us on this side of the table. And that was an effective

24   force. And I can tell you for a fact, because I saw it with

25   my own eyes, I saw battalion commanders, brigade commanders,

1   and division commanders distinguish themselves in combat and

2   under significant stress. And we felt good about that

3   force. We were saying, "Wow, they finally -- they've got it

4   together." What happened to that force? Well, so much

5   attention has been placed on Maliki's malice in what he did

6   to undermine his political opponents. He destroyed that

7   force, because he saw those distinguished leaders, who were

8   accomplished as a result of their performance on the

9   battlefield, and their people were devoted to them -- he saw

10   them as threats to him, politically as well as his political

11   opponents. And he undermined that force. He purged that

12   force.

13   So, that force is not there, the one that we used to

14   have. He put in these political phonies and cranks and

15   other people who didn't have the military competence. Well,

16   that -- changing leadership and getting that leadership

17   back, and others who are willing to have that kind of

18   commitment and competence, that takes a little time to fix.

19   But, the fact that we did have it, Senator, at one time, and

20   it was pretty good, tells you that there is something there

21   that we can work with, and we can get it back there.

22   Whether that can be done in time is another issue.

23   Senator King: Looks around -- I may be the chair now,

24   so I'm going to give myself another 10 seconds.

25   One simple question, though. In 2007-2008, how many

1   Americans were in Iraq?

2   General Keane: Certainly. I mean, we had somewhere in

3   the neighborhood -- correct me if I'm wrong, guys -- about

4   130,000 in Iraq. And that's how that force grew to the --

5   but, what I'm saying to you is that, when we finished, when

6   we had completed our involvement in Iraq, the force that

7   we'd left there was a capable force, the Iraqi Security

8   Force.

9   Senator King: I understand that. The question is,

10 What do we have to do to rebuild it? That's the question.

11   I'm out of time.

12   Senator Sullivan [presiding]: Thank you, Mr. Chair.

13   Gentlemen, thank you for your testimony.

14   I wanted to talk at -- initially, about the issue of

15 credibility. And, you know, there's been a lot of

16 discussion about how we've lost credibility with our allies

17 in places like Syria. But, I also want to talk about the

18 importance of the issue of credibility with the American

19 people. And there has been, I think, a narrative in the

20 administration that has not been helpful, in that there's

21 been an emphasis on the fact that we are now -- our combat

22 role in the Middle East is now finished. Well, of course,

23 it isn't finished. Just tell that to the pilots who are

24 flying daily missions. We think of combat in terms of the

25 infantry soldiers, but a lot of times we forget the brave

1   men and women who are flying these missions, daily. And

2   they're -- that's combat. And obviously, also, with the

3   recent Delta Force mission by some very brave Americans,

4   that's boots on the ground. So, we're in combat. We even

5   have boots on the ground, but there's still this narrative

6   that somehow we're done.

7   So, General Keane, what I wanted to ask you, first of

8   all, is, Do you think that this narrative, which is a false

9   one, in my view, has inhibited our ability to actually

10   develop a robust strategy we're talking about? Do we need

11   JTACs, do we need other forces on the ground? And yet,

12   we're competing with a narrative from the White House that

13   says, "No, no, no, no, we're done." And it seems to me that

14   would be a limiting factor to developing a strategy that

15   ultimately is -- would do what we all want it to do, which

16   is protect America's national security interests.

17   General Keane: Well, yes, I certainly -- when I look

18   at it and try to speculate about what is driving some of our

19   decisions, what is driving our narrative, you know, one of

20   the things I've observed since I've been closer to it in

21   recent years than when I was when I was a younger officer,

22   is that most administrations, Democratic or Republican, have

23   a tendency to overreact to what took place in the previous

24   administration. And I think this one is no exception to

25   that, making a -- making it a principle of the

1   administration to have a guarantor that we will not be

2   involved in any military activity in the Middle East or in

3   South Asia that could lead to another protracted war. And I

4   think that's probably good -- a good principle. But, the

5   issue is, that should not trump what's necessary to do,

6   given the fact that ISIS represents a new organization --

7   Senator Sullivan: Yeah.

8   General Keane: -- with new leadership, a new vision,

9   in terms of its global and regional strategy, and that it is

10   a barbaric organization committing genocide, assassination,

11   enslavement of women, and raping of women, as we all know,

12   and that it is fully intent on conducting a religious war

13   based on their ideology. And we cannot let the rearview

14   mirror of Iraq and Afghanistan so disincentivize us to deal

15   with the reality of what this is. And I'm convinced that

16   the American people, when we inform them --

17   Senator Sullivan: Yeah.

18   General Keane: -- and we educate them, and we take

19   them through this -- I mean, I dealt with the Bush

20   administration. They never truly explained what radical

21   Islam is and why it was so dangerous. We never truly took

22   apart the ideology.

23   Senator Sullivan: Yeah.

24   General Keane: We never truly fashioned a strategy to

25   deal with it in a comprehensive way.

1   Senator Sullivan: Can I -- I'd like to follow up --

2   General Keane: And here we sit, with the same problem

3   today.

4   Senator Sullivan: I think that's a great point, and

5   it's something that I think -- my own view is that you're

6   directly on point. If we level with the American people,

7   talk about the threats, talk about the strategy, that --

8   it's really important -- many of you have been raising that

9   -- I think everybody recognizes what we -- you know, once we

10   lay that out, what we would or wouldn't have to do to

11   address it.

12   So, let me ask a kind of a related question for Mr.

13   Kagan. You've written on the long war, the idea of -- that

14   I think sometimes we look at what's going on with ISIS and

15   other issues in the Middle East and think, "Hey, we're going

16   to have this done in a couple of months -- 18 months, 20

17   months, maybe a couple of years." Do you think that there

18   is an importance to having the leadership, both in terms of

19   Congress, but particularly the executive branch, talk more

20   broadly -- and again, level with the American people --

21   about that this might be a generational conflict, this might

22   be akin to the Cold War, where we've got to lay out a broad

23   strategy -- and, Mr. Katulis, I think your point, early on

24   in your testimony, about the need for a strategic concept is

25   so important -- lay out a strategy that the executive

1   branch, the legislative branch, and the American people can

2   get behind, and then execute it. And level with the

3   American people that this might not be done in 18 months.

4   So, would any of you care -- Mr. Kagan, I know you've

5   written about the long war. Could you -- would you feel

6   free to talk about that?

7   And, Mr. Katulis, I'd be very interested -- when you

8   talked about the strategic concept. What is it? Obviously,

9   20 seconds left, that's a big topic. But, if you could

10 point us in the direction of your writings or some

11 principles that all of you have thought about, I think that

12 would be very helpful.

13   Mr. Kagan?

14   Dr. Kagan: Senator, I mean, this is a generational

15 struggle that we're in, at least. It may be longer than --

16   Senator Sullivan: But, we don't talk about it that

17 way, do we --

18   Dr. Kagan: No, on the --

19   Senator Sullivan: -- very much?

20   Dr. Kagan: -- contrary. I think your first -- the

21 point that you opened with is a very important one, that

22 when the administration's narrative is that we're ending the

23 wars, it is impossible to develop an -- a coherent strategy

24 for fighting the wars. And we do need to understand that

25 this is a war. This is -- these are battle fronts on a

1   common war that is going to last for a long time. And we

2   don't get to end it unless we win. But, you don't get to

3   decide -- we may not be interested in war, but war is

4   interested in us. And this is going to continue to be a

5   problem. And we need to level with the American people, as

6   you say, as a basis for developing any kind of strategy. I

7   totally agree with you.

8   Mr. Katulis: I think we need to define what we want to

9   achieve. Quite often over the last 14 years, in

10   Afghanistan, in Iraq, now with ISIL, we define our

11   objectives in terms of what we're going to counter and

12   defeat. That's important. But, what has been missing, I

13   think, comprehensively, whether it's in a particular

14   theater, like Iraq or Syria or Afghanistan, is the

15   definition of what we actually need to leave behind in those

16   societies, how we help others help themselves.

17   I do believe, at certain points -- President Bush

18   certainly did this; certain points, President Obama does

19   this -- talks about the long-term nature of this. If you

20   look at their planning documents, at least, for the anti-

21   ISIL strategy, it doesn't say, "Let's end this." As the

22   administration used to say about Afghanistan and Iraq,

23   "We're going to end it at a particular period of time." It

24   extends into who will be the next President.

25   But, your point is terribly important, and I have

1 written several articles and a book about this, too. It's

 2 important, because, for our own society, there is a new

 3 generation, called Millennials, that are actually, this

 4 year, in number, larger than the Baby Boomers or -- I'm a

 5 Generation X-er. Our leaders aren't messaging in a cohesive

 6 way. And I think part of it is the partisanship that we

 7 have in our politics and other things. And I -- I'm a

 8 strong centrist internationalist. I believe that we need to

 9 bring the American people along with us.

10   And something Senator Kaine has said here earlier and

11 before is that the debate that we need to be having on the

12 authorization of the use of military force, and action on it

13 -- this is a moment which has not been seized. You could

14 criticize the administration or you could criticize whomever

15 in Congress. There's been this muddle. And I think part of

16 the reason, it goes back to, we actually haven't defined for

17 the American public, in the way that Fred and others have

18 argued here, that the U.S. has a special leadership role in

19 the world. Our leadership -- countries in the region are

20 still looking to us to actually do more. But, we need to

21 actually take those steps beyond the questions on military

22 and security steps, which are terribly important. We need

23 to actually, then, talk about, How do we defeat these

24 ideologies? We've done it before, with Naziism or

25 Communism. You know, they're on the margins. Our model is

1 much better. Our values are better. But, what happened to

2 the battle of ideas? We had that debate for a couple of

3 years after 9/11. We kind of rediscovered it for a little

4 bit. But, I think our ADD, our attention deficit disorder,

5 in our own society -- and that's what I would say is, as

6 thought leaders, as leaders in Congress, we all have a

7 responsibility to continue to talk about this in a sustained

8 way.

9   Senator Sullivan: Thank you.

10   Thank you, gentlemen.

11   Senator Kaine [presiding]: We've all had one round,

12 but if anybody has a second round -- I'm just going to seize

13 the moment, here, to continue for a few minutes, if we can.

14   I'm interested -- we've had visits in the Senate

15 Foreign Relations from leaders that are our allies -- King

16 -- the King of Jordan, in January; the Emir of Qatar, in

17 February. We've had discussions with Saudi leadership,

18 including the Saudi Ambassador. And every time we have

19 these discussions, I ask them, "Tell us what you think the

20 role of the U.S. should be, vis-a-vis ISIL, the battle

21 against ISIL." And, in particular, because this is a point

22 of difference among some on the Foreign Relations Committee,

23 I've asked about the -- their thought about American ground

24 troops. And I want to tell you what they've said, but then

25 I'm curious about your opinions about what they've said.

1   The King of Jordan said, "That would be a mistake.

2   This is our battle, not yours. And if it gets positioned as

3   the U.S. against ISIL, then that will not be a helpful

4   thing. If it's -- we stand up against the terrorist threat

5   in our own region, and the U.S. helps us in a vigorous way,

6   but clearly a supporter, not the main driver, that's the way

7   this should position, and significant U.S. ground troops

8   would -- just like the U.S. is doing 90 percent of the

9   airstrikes, the significant U.S. ground troops would make

10   this the U.S. against ISIL."

11   The Emir of Qatar said, similarly, "If there's

12   significant ground troop presence from the United States,

13   this will be the -- a recruiting bonanza for ISIL."

14   In Saudi Arabia -- and this -- the meetings with the

15   Saudis occurred right after the Saudis had gone in a major

16   way into Yemen, but -- so, they're -- you know, they're

17   willing, at least somewhere, to take some significant

18   military action to deal with threats in their own region,

19   but they also said, "U.S. ground troops against ISIL would

20   be problematic."

21   Now, I don't -- you know, I'm not -- I didn't read that

22   to say, "not even one," or "under no circumstances." But,

23   they were very wary about the notion of U.S. ground troops.

24   So, we're trying to work that out on the Foreign

25   Relations Committee as we think about an authorization. Are

1   they right? Are they wrong? Of, if they're right, how

2   would you square that with what a U.S. presence, U.S.

3   support should mean?

4   Mr. Katulis: If I could start. It's why I -- the

5   thrust of my remarks were on this coalition.

6   I actually think, for all of the criticisms of the

7   Obama administration's strategy, some of which I share, this

8   is the one component that simply did not exist before. It's

9   one that has been underutilized, I believe. I do think that

10 things like the GCC Summit last week, though there were a

11 lot of optics and news articles about it, there is a

12 conversation to try to build on, What can we do in

13 partnership with them?

14   So, I think if there's one thing we should have learned

15 from 2003 to 2010 or '11 in Iraq, is that, yes, U.S. forces

16 can have an important impact on the security situation

17 there. But, there's also downsides to having such a visible

18 presence.

19   I don't think anyone on the panel -- unless I misheard

20 it -- was talking about ever going back to, say, a 2006-2007

21 posture. But, I do think striking the right balance is the

22 key question. I think the administration has been

23 understandably reticent about what it does in Iraq,

24 Afghanistan, Syria, and other places, given the unforced

25 errors on the part of the United States. But, this regional

1   dynamic has shifted quite a lot, which is what I was trying

2   to emphasize.

3   The region, itself, recognizes that the U.S., in a very

4   visible presence on the ground, does have significant

5   downsides for their own legitimacy with their own

6   populations. The region also is taking action in what it

7   sees as its own self-interest. What I was trying to say, in

8   terms of a multidimensional -- it's not only security

9   support; it's investment in media campaigns and different

10 political forces across the region.

11   Where I think the U.S. strategy right now -- and again,

12 it's more honed in on what my expertise and focus is --

13 where we need to enhance it more is working with those

14 reliable partners, from Jordan to the United Arab Emirates

15 to Saudi Arabia to a number of different allies, including

16 the Kurds we've talked about, and some of the Iraqis, to

17 actually take what has been a significantly larger amount of

18 resources in energy and activity and channel it towards more

19 constructive purposes. I don't see that happening in Yemen

20 right now. I don't see that happening yet in Syria. And I

21 don't see that happening in many other theaters.

22   So, I think the basic answer to the question -- the

23 leaders that you spoke with, I think, are reflecting a very

24 popular view at the popular level in their countries, as

25 well. They understand that, for whatever happened in the

1   Iraq War, the surge, and other things, the U.S. is better

2   sort of seen as a backbone of support behind them, as

3   opposed to visibly out in the front.

4   Dr. Kagan: Senator, I think we need to distinguish

5   between the ideal and reality. Ideally, of course it would

6   be better for regional states to take care of regional

7   problems, and regional militaries to be involved, with a

8   caveat that we do have a regional war going on, and the

9   regional actors we're talking about are being seen as on one

10 side of that. So, we need to think about what the Iranian

11 reaction would be to Saudi divisions deploying into Iraq on

12 behalf of the Iraqis. I don't think we would enjoy that

13 very much. And I think it might be worse, actually, than

14 the Iranian reaction to the deployment of U.S. forces in

15 there. So, it's a complicated dynamic.

16   But, look, in the world of reality, the Jordanians,

17 they don't have the forces to do this. The Saudis don't

18 have -- the regional militaries are not capable of providing

19 the kind of assistance to Iraq that we can provide. They

20 don't have it in their force structure, they don't have it

21 in their --

22   Senator Kaine: How about the Turks?

23   Dr. Kagan: The Turks might be able to provide some

24 element of it, although no one provides the capability that

25 the U.S. provides to its allies, including the Turks, and

1   they would still be dependent on us.

2   But, again, the -- I'm really not sure that the optics

3   of the return of the Ottoman Empire in force to Iraq would

4   be better than the optics of having a limited number of

5   American troops on the ground there. So, I think that the

6   regional leaders you're talking to are expressing an ideal

7   version of a strategy which we would all like to see, but

8   it's not in accord with reality.

9   And, as you think about an AUMF, I would say an AUMF in

10 which Congress micromanages what forces can or cannot be

11 sent, and thereby, in my opinion, infringes somewhat on the

12 prerogative of the President to choose how to fight a war

13 that Congress authorizes, but also, in this circumstances,

14 that would constrain the deployment of American ground

15 forces when they are so clearly necessary, would be

16 extremely damaging.

17   Colonel Harvey: Senator Kaine, if I could.

18   This reminds me of the myth that I heard in Iraq about:

19 U.S. forces were the generator of the antibodies that caused

20 the insurgency. It was a real misreading of what was going

21 on in Iraq in the drivers of the fight.

22   We have to be focused on what are U.S. interests and

23 how do we defeat this enemy. And the seeds of strategic

24 failure are found in failing to define that enemy, define

25 our interests, the costs, and the risks. And if we do those

1   things, and we think about our interests, it will drive us

2   to engage more seriously than we have, in my mind. I think

3   it's a very similar situation today. We study

4   radicalization, recruitment for the foreign fighter flow.

5   The U.S. presence in Iraq is not going to dramatically

6   increase the foreign fighter flow. It is being driven by a

7   range of issues and the different types of recruits that are

8   being pulled in from Tunisia and elsewhere. The driver

9   within Iraq is not the U.S. presence, it's Shi'a domination,

10 it's the fear for their future and their own lives and lack

11 of political inclusion, et cetera. That's the issue we need

12 to get our head around.

13   General Keane: Yeah, I -- you know, I agree with what

14 everybody's said here. And I think we talk past each other

15 a little bit on this issue. No one here, certainly, is

16 advocating that we should have ground units that are

17 occupying towns and villages, and securing them, and

18 therefore, protecting them from ISIS attack that would put

19 us right in the mainstream of defending against ISIS. Now,

20 I think that's unnecessary, and it would be a mistake. But

21 also, when we have a policy that says "no boots on the

22 ground," that doesn't make any sense, either, because it

23 denies us from having advisors that have a role to play, it

24 denies us with -- from forward air controllers that have a

25 role to play, as we pointed out, and other military

1   capabilities that are unique to us. And we've elaborated on

2   what they are. They are significant enablers that make --

3   would make a difference in what the 60 nations have agreed

4   to do, which is support the Iraqi ground forces, as

5   imperfect as they are. But, let's give them a better hand

6   to play than what we are doing. And I don't believe there

7   is a single nation that would object to anything of what we

8   are describing is -- are enablers that would make a

9   difference.

10   Second, when it comes to Syria, I think this is a

11   difference. And if you spoke to them about that, you know

12   what their view is about Assad. We've already dealt with

13   that in the regime. And they know full well that the deal

14   with ISIS in Syria, this is going to take a ground force,

15   and they would have to contribute to that ground force. I

16   would think that they would logically ask us to participate

17   in that with them. We would -- I don't think we would

18   necessarily have to be the largest contributor, but I think

19   we would have to participate. And I think they would

20   reasonably want us, too, because of our experience and our

21   capabilities, if we would actually lead it. Maybe not.

22   But, I think those two things would probably be on the

23   table for discussion. And I think it's reasonable that that

24   kind of allocation of U.S. capability and leadership to deal

25   with ISIS in Syria is, in fact, an eventuality.

1   Senator Kaine: Senator Blumenthal, do you have

2   questions for the panel?

3   Senator Blumenthal: I do. Thank you very much.

4   Thank you all for being here and for your very

5   thoughtful and eloquent remarks. I was here for the

6   beginning remarks. Unfortunately, as so often happens here,

7   I was diverted to another committee meeting after our vote.

8   I want to come back to what Mr. Kagan was describing as

9   the "evil" of ISIS/ISIL and the absolutely horrid,

10   unspeakable acts of brutality that they commit -- mass rape,

11   mass murder. And I agree with you that they are one of the

12   most evil, maybe the most evil institution in history. We

13   can argue about it. But, when I go home this weekend, most

14   folks are going to ask me, What's the threat to the United

15   States? And 50 years from now, others will be sitting where

16   you are, and where I am, talking about probably other evil

17   institutions that are committing mass brutality. Because

18   that seems to be, unfortunately and tragically, the nature

19   of the human condition. It's happened throughout our

20   history. And I think the ordinary person in Connecticut

21   over the Memorial Day weekend is going to wonder what our

22   role should be in stopping that from occurring unless there

23   is a threat to this country. So, perhaps you and others on

24   the panel could tell me what I should tell the people of

25   Connecticut about why the United States should be involved,

1   whether it is Special Operations Forces or better air

2   support or whatever the involvement is, and why that matters

3   to our security.

4   Dr. Kagan: Senator, I think it's a fair question.

5   And, as a Connecticut native, I'm -- I am concerned about

6   what you have to tell the Connecticut people to get them

7   onboard with this.

8   May I start by saying -- as I was driving down to

9   Virginia the other day, I drove past the Holocaust Museum,

10   and I saw, again, the sign that's up there that is always

11   there, which is "Never Again." And I would submit that we

12   need -- one of the things we need to tell the American

13   people is that America is not historically a country that

14   watches these kinds of atrocities on this scale occur and

15   does nothing. It actually is a core American value to take

16   a stand against these kind of -- we do it very late, we did

17   -- we try to talk ourselves out of it, we have long

18   arguments about it, but, ultimately, we generally do it.

19   And that's one of the things that makes us America. And I

20   think we really shouldn't lose sight of that moral

21   imperative as we talk about this.

22   But, your comments are very well taken, sir. The

23   reality is, ISIS poses a clear and present danger to the

24   United States homeland. It has already been encouraging,

25   condoning, and applauding lone-wolf attacks here. It has

1   made it clear that it has the objective of attacking America
2   and the West, that it is actively recruiting cells in
3   America and the West. And it will do that with the
4   resources of a ministate behind it, which is something that
5   we have never seen before with al-Qaeda. This is not a
6   group of bandits hanging out in the mountains in
7   Afghanistan. And that attack was devastating enough. But,
8   if we reflect on the resources that ISIS has access to,
9   controlling Mosul, Fallujah, Ramadi, al-Raqqa, oil
10   infrastructure, the resources that were in various
11   universities in Mosul and so forth, that -- thousands of
12   fighters, tens of thousands of recruits -- this is an army,
13   and this is an army that is very sophisticated and has an
14   ability to conduct operational military planning and execute
15   it that is in advance of anything that I've seen from any of
16   these groups. And it has declared its intention to come
17   after the United States, and shown a willingness to do that.
18   That is something that I think the people of Connecticut
19   need to be concerned about.
20   General Keane: Yeah, I would certainly agree with what
21   Fred is saying, is that it should be a concern to us, in a
22   couple of ways. Certainly, what they are doing to motivate
23   and inspire others who are not necessarily in the region but
24   are in other countries and are -- can identify with this
25   movement, and many of them are self-radicalized or possibly

they're already radicalized, but they're motivated to take
action, and take violent action. We've seen plenty of
evidence of that.

    And the longer you permit the organization to succeed
-- can you imagine what has gone out on the Internet from
ISIS around the world as a result of their success in
Ramadi, and how that has motivated others, that ISIS, in
fact, is winning, and they're standing up against the United
States, they're standing up against these strong allies of
the United States in the region and Europe, and they're
actually winning? So, there's huge danger there. As long
as you let this organization stay and we don't decapitate
it, then they -- the motivation and inspiration of self-
radicalization continues to grow. That's one thing.

    The second thing is, in the region itself -- and we
showed on a map -- they're moving into other countries at
the same time they're defending what they have in Syria and
Iraq, and expanding in those countries. This is what makes
this organization so very different than what we've dealt
with in the past. And they're looking at Libya as a --
because of the social and political upheaval in Libya -- and
there's hardly a government there and anybody to push back
on it -- they're going to put huge resources in there. Why
are we concerned about that? Our interests in the region,
our interests in North Africa, that would be on the southern

1   tip of NATO there, not too many miles away from Italy. In

2   Afghanistan, they have expanded rapidly, beyond most of our

3   expectations, I would assume, into eight provinces in

4   Afghanistan. Now, we have interests in Afghanistan, for

5   obvious reasons.

6   So, this is a movement that we can tie directly to the

7   security of the American people and to our national security

8   objectives of the United States in this region and in South

9   Asia.

10   Senator Blumenthal: So, it -- if I can put it a

11 different way, just to conclude, it's more than -- and, by

12 the way, American values are directly and inevitably linked

13 to stopping human atrocities. I agree totally with you, Mr.

14 Kagan. But, our interests go beyond that -- those values.

15 And, by the way, all of the reasons that you've articulated

16 are the reasons that I voted for the training and equipping

17 measures that have been implemented. But, my frustration is

18 that, as you also have observed, there is a huge gap between

19 the goals and missions that we've outlined for the United

20 States and the actual action that we're undertaking. The

21 train-and-equip activities are way behind what we might have

22 hoped by this point, and there's no clear timetable for

23 really achieving the level of capability that we expected or

24 hoped.

25   So, I think this has been a very sobering morning, and

1   I thank you all for being here.

2   Thank you.

3   Chairman McCain [presiding]: Well, I also want to

4   thank the witnesses. And it's been, I think, very helpful

5   to all members. And this is not an issue that's going away.

6   So, I'm sure that we'll be seeing you again.

7   Thank you.

8   This hearing is adjourned.

9   [Whereupon, at 11:59 a.m., the hearing was adjourned.]

10

11

12

13

14

15

16

17

18

19

20

21

22

23

24

25

www.ingramcontent.com/pod-product-compliance
Lightning Source LLC
Chambersburg PA
CBHW080417290526
45791CB00008BA/2318